THE KURDISH QUASI-STATE

Modern Intellectual and Political History of the Middle East
Mehrzad Boroujerdi, *Series Editor*

THE
KURDISH
QUASI-STATE

Development and Dependency
in Post–Gulf War Iraq

DENISE NATALI

SYRACUSE UNIVERSITY PRESS

ISBN: 978-0-8156-3217-7

Library of Congress Cataloging-in-Publication Data

Natali, Denise.

   The Kurdish quasi-state : development and dependency in post–Gulf War Iraq /
Denise Natali. — 1st ed.

      p. cm. — (Modern intellectual and political history of the Middle East)

   Includes bibliographical references and index.

   ISBN 978-0-8156-3217-7 (cloth : alk. paper)

   1. Kurds—Iraq—Politics and government—20th century.   2. Kurds—Iraq—Politics
and government—21st century.   3. Kurdistan (Iraq)—Politics and government—20th
century.   4. Kurdistan (Iraq)—Politics and government—21st century.   5. Kurdistan
(Iraq)—Foreign relations.   6. Economic assistance—Iraq—Kurdistan.   7. Military
assistance—Iraq—Kurdistan.   I. Title.

   DS70.8.K8N37 2010

   956.7'20443—dc22   2010017116

For Héline

Denise Natali is Research Centers director and associate professor at the American University of Iraq–Sulaimania. She is the author of numerous publications on Kurdish nationalism, politics, and identity, including *The Kurds and the State: Evolving National Identity in Iraq, Turkey, and Iran* (Syracuse University Press, 2005). Dr. Natali also has worked in disaster relief and post-conflict reconstruction programs in Washington, D.C.; Peshwar, Pakistan; and post–Gulf War Iraqi Kurdistan.

Contents

Illustrations

Tables

Preface

WHEN I FIRST TRAVELED to the Kurdistan Region of Iraq in 1992 it was to analyze the controversial election outcomes that created the first Kurdistan Regional Government (KRG). Socioeconomic conditions at that time were as unstable as the newly created parliament. There was no food in the markets, no salaries for civil servants, and no facilities in which to resettle the hundreds of thousands of refugees and internally displaced persons (IDPs) in the region. The Kurdish *peshmerga* (militia) had just descended from its mountain strongholds after decades of fighting against the central government and rival Kurdish parties. A culture of Kalashnikovs still permeated the streets and bazaars.

No one would have imagined back then that the isolated and unstable Kurdistan Region would have become one of the most viable areas of the country. Nor could it have been realistically envisioned that the once unrecognized KRG would have assumed a key role in keeping Iraq together and ensuring regional stability. Had the Kurdish north remained in the civil war that shook the region from 1994 to 1998, then the contemporary political and economic situation probably would have been easier to explain.

Most perplexing are the changes that have occurred in the region and the contradictions they pose to popular discourses about an independent and highly autonomous Kurdistan. Many people saw—and still see—the creation of a safe haven and subsequent development processes as a precursor to Kurdish statehood. They interpreted the "booming" post-Saddam Kurdistan Region as one that would eventually become self-sustaining and not need to remain attached to the dysfunctional Iraqi state. Underlying this view is the assumption that Kurdish state-building is a linear process, a function of unchanging and deep-rooted nationalist sentiment, or causally related to the weak Iraqi central government.

This image of Kurdish nationalism and state building comes into question, however, when focusing on the political economy of post-conflict regions and the realities of quasi-state survival. In post-Saddam Iraq, where social, economic, and political transformations have given the KRG new rights, recognition, and revenues, the Kurdish nationalist agenda coincides with the overriding need for development and stability. The Kurds must now choose between electricity and independence, international legitimacy and pan-Kurdish nationalism, and external patronage and extended territorial claims. Their political decisions are no longer largely driven by nationalist fervor, but by how to keep borders to their landlocked region continuously open and protected, how to attract international investment, and how to pacify the increasingly disgruntled local populations demanding basic services and good governance.

The more I heard and read about "potential Kurdish statehood," the more I wanted to explain the emergence and sustainability of the Kurdish quasi-state over time. Rooted in wishful thinking or misplaced fear, and linked to outdated stereotypes and nationalist jargon, the independent statehood discourse discounted the important changes that had occurred in the region and their impact on promoting or constraining stability. Not surprisingly, misunderstandings about the Kurdish quasi-state and its place in Iraq festered.

While acknowledging historical legacies and ethno-nationalist sentiment that have shaped the Kurdistan Region over time, this book focuses on external factors, and particularly on foreign aid, as providing the necessary foundation to create and sustain Kurdish quasi-statehood. Part of this influence certainly has been negative. During my tenure as information officer for the US Office of Foreign Disaster Assistance (OFDA) in Iraqi Kurdistan during the early 1990s, I saw the unintentional consequences of foreign aid on the local political economy: imbalances in the distribution of resources, power struggles between rival groups, competition for revenues, and civil war. In many cases the most needy never even received aid, and if they did, it was only temporarily, before they sold their goods in the bazaar. Still, the generous nature of external aid to the Kurdistan Region over time created numerous opportunity structures that encouraged stability and set the groundwork for political and economic development. Had foreign assistance not been continuously available to willing aid recipients, the postwar trajectory of the Kurdistan Region may have had a very different outcome.

The focus on the role of external aid comes at a time of criticisms of U.S. intervention in Iraq and debates about U.S. troop withdrawal from the country. By taking a detailed and deep look at the spoils of peace in the Kurdish north, this book challenges the notion of the futility of U.S. intervention and shows some of the positive influences foreign assistance has had on the transition to peace. External aid not only has encouraged the development and relative stability of the Kurdish quasi-state, but also has helped assure that it remains a part of Iraq.

I would like to thank the American Academic Research Institute in Iraq (TAARI) for its financial support of this project from a 2005–6 research grant award. I also thank Exeter University's Institute for Arab and Islamic Studies, the University of Salahaddin, and the University of Kurdistan (UKH) in Arbil for providing administrative and research support while I was researching and writing this book in the Kurdistan Region of Iraq in 2005–2009. Many students and young people willingly assisted me inside and outside the classroom with their open ideas, enthusiasm, and insights. I am most appreciative to Namo Kalary, Hemin Hussein, Mohammed Ali Bapir, Hakim Qadir Taha Herany, Hardy Shukir, Tawfiq Rahman, Singar Musa, and Husam Algilly for their comprehensive research assistance. I thank numerous friends and colleagues, including Mohammed Towfiq, Hawre Riwandizi, Nariman Ali, and Ralph Gonzales for offering their generous time to discuss politics and security and economic issues, and for offering me access to necessary contacts and information networks.

Edward Luttwak, Ian Lustick, Eric Davis, Henri Barkey, Zafer Yöruk, Francis Owtram, and two anonymous reviewers made important comments and critiques of different proposals, chapters, and drafts of the manuscript. Participants at the Durham University's Department of Government and International Affairs Conference on the Politics of Virtual States and the National Defense University's Conference on Iraqi Elections offered invaluable insights and suggestions that improved the content and argument of the book.

I thank the Emirates Center for Strategic Studies and Research (ECSSR) and Routledge (Taylor and Francis Group) for permission to reprint parts of earlier publications from which sections of this book have been drawn.

Most important, I thank my daughter, Héline, for her patience and support during this research project, which involved numerous shuttles from Paris to Arbil and extended absences that have become part of ordinary family life.

Héline, who was only five when she first went with me on the first commercial flight from Europe to the Kurdistan Region, willingly rode the local buses and taxis, patiently sat through dozens of interviews, traveled to the villages, meandered through the bazaars with me, and learned Kurdish and some Arabic along the way. I could not have written this book without her or the inspiration she gave me during the process.

Abbreviations

ADM	Assyrian Democratic Movement
BMEO	British Middle East Office
DOD	Department of Defense
FAO	Food and Agricultural Organization
IBRD	International Bank for Reconstruction and Development
IDP	internally displaced person
IKP	Iraqi Kurdistan Parliament
IMK	Islamic Movement of Kurdistan
INC	Iraqi National Congress
INGO	international nongovernmental organization
IRFFI	International Reconstruction Fund Facility for Iraq
ISD	Iraqi Swiss dinar
KDP	Kurdistan Democratic Party
KF	Kurdistan Front
KNA	Kurdistan National Assembly
KRG	Kurdistan Regional Government
MCC	Military Coordination Center
MERA	Ministry of Extra-Regional Affairs
MORAD	Ministry of Reconstruction and Development
MOU	Memorandum of Understanding
MT	metric ton
NGO	nongovernmental organization

NID	New Iraqi dinar
OFDA	Office of Foreign Disaster Assistance
OFFP	Oil for Food Programme
OID	Old Iraqi dinar
OPC	Operation Provide Comfort
PKK	Partîye Karkâren Kurdistane
PUK	Patriotic Union of Kurdistan
PVO	private voluntary organization
UN	United Nations
UNDP	United Nations Development Programme
UNHCR	United Nations High Commissioner for Refugees
UNICEF	United Nations Children's Fund
UNOHCI	The United Nations Office of the Humanitarian Coordinator in Iraq
USAID	United States Agency for International Development
WFP	World Food Programme
WMD	weapons of mass destruction

Introduction

Aiding Quasi-States

SINCE THE 1990 PERSIAN GULF WAR, the political economy of Iraq has been marked by a breakdown of state authority, criminality, and socioeconomic deterioration. War entrepreneurs circumvented the internationally imposed sanctions regime (UNSCR 687) by instrumentalizing humanitarian aid and creating new forms of wealth, inequalities, and patronage (Barnett, Eggleston, and Webber 2003; Looney 2003a, 2; Graham-Brown 2002, 277–78; Griffiths 1999, 68; Pugh 2002; Jean 1996, 579–89). Predation continued after the overthrow of Saddam Hussein and the Ba'athist government in 2003, further reducing the possibilities of a transition to sustainable peace. Yet, despite the rent-seeking behavior pervasive in postwar Iraq, transition patterns have varied across the country. Whereas the southern and central governorates have become mired in civil war and economic stagnation, the Kurdish north, historically one of Iraq's most unstable and underdeveloped areas, has experienced relative stability and certain levels of development. What explains the transition path in Iraqi Kurdistan, what is the nature of the transformations, and how has it influenced the relationship between the Kurdistan Region[1] and the central government?

---

1. The Kurdistan Region includes those territories administered by the Kurdistan Regional Government (KRG) in the governorates of Suleymaniya, Dohuk, and Arbil. Discussions between the KRG and the Iraqi central government continue to decide jurisdiction of disputed territories inside the present-day governorates of Kirkuk, Ninevah (Mosul), Diyala, and Wasit (Kut). They are "disputed" because they have been subjected to changes in internal boundaries, administrative units, resources, and demographics as part of the central government's larger Arabization program.

This book examines the extent to which externally driven aid has had an impact on the Kurdistan Region and the influence of these transformations on Kurdish-state relations. It aims to show that while structural legacies and ethnic traditions have historically defined the relationship between the Kurds and the central government, external aid has created new dependencies and interdependencies, and avenues for conflict and cooperation. A key variable is the nature of aid, which can change over time and have different consequences on local development and political processes (Anderson 1999, 34). Aid programs can favor some groups over others, create new linkages within and between regions, and enforce rivalries where they may not have arisen.

In post–Gulf War Iraqi Kurdistan, for instance, the external aid program has shifted from short-term relief to development to reconstruction within a neoliberal framework. While advancing Kurdish autonomy, it has encouraged the creation of entrepreneurial classes and a more diversified workforce, and has enhanced trade between the Kurdistan Region, regional states, and foreign governments (Looney 2003a). Greater complexity in the political economy is expected to support economic growth, interdependence, and opportunities for compromise, alongside challenges of Kurdish ethnonationalism. Asymmetrical growth can also influence center-periphery relations by strengthening the Kurdistan Region's political power in relation to the state and increasing leverage on the central government to accommodate Kurdish demands (Bookman 1991).

Indeed, the argument of aid influencing post-conflict development is not a new one. Whether emphasizing aid policies, program implementation, the distributional impacts of aid, or the economics of peacemaking, most studies reveal that post-conflict states cannot commence recovery processes without long-term international aid and donor support (Knack 2004, 251–52; Brynen 2000, 19; Anderson 1999, 34–44; Gounder 2002; Deely 2005, 123). Still, the effect of particular types of foreign aid regimes across space and time is unclear. Relief aid based on direct handouts may alleviate immediate needs and help stabilize post-conflict disasters; however, it can negatively affect development by giving aid recipients no stake in planning or implementation. Generous foreign assistance can reduce the need for governments to tax their citizens, which can decrease government accountability and the rule of law while encouraging the politics of dependency (Jones 2005, 107; Knack 2004, 253; Billet 1993, 98; Rondinelli 1987, 3). In contrast, assistance grounded in capacity building—development aimed at strengthening the infrastructure beyond earlier conditions—can establish institutions, develop social capital, spur economic growth, and support linkages between foreign governments and nonstate actors (Brynen 2000, 19, 28–29; Anderson 1999, 34–44; Gounder 2002; Hout 2004, 595; MacLean 2004; Ball 1996; Collier et al. 2003; Blomberg and Hess 2002; Peck 1998, 45).

Even then, the nature of external aid is tied to broader international politics and the strategic interests of donor agencies, which can have different effects on development policy, programs, and outcomes (Macrae 2001, 7; Zaborowski 2005, 23; Hout 2004, 600). Reconstruction of post–World War II Eastern Europe, for instance, focused on industrialization, neglected agriculture, and channeled aid through political parties and the state apparatus and not individuals. In Western Europe the Marshall Plan was tied to state building, norms of participation, self-sustainability, stabilizing currencies and exchange rates, and conducting regular reviews of aid (Barakat 2005, 15–18). For least-developing countries (LDCs) in the 1970s, external aid focused on short-term needs of relieving hunger and not long-term development. Liberalization programs in the former state-run Soviet states altered market relations, encouraged urbanization, and destabilized social structures. In Somalia the primary goal was to create a framework for security and human rights and to promote economic liberalization and constitutional reform (Macrae 2001, 88).

The influence of foreign aid becomes further complicated when examining quasi-states, or unrecognized de facto or semi-states. Quasi-states are political entities that have internal but not external sovereignty and seek some form of autonomy or independence. They are part of a failed state or an outcome of unfair postimperial boundary markers (Chorev 2007, 4–18; 37; Kolsto 2006, 724).[2] Quasi-statehood can also apply to statelike entities such as rebel movements that control territory and carry out statelike functions but lack the juridical status of sovereign governments (Macrae 2001, 4). Aiding quasi-states involves distinct processes because of the highly politicized context in which foreign assistance is implemented. Studies of Palestine show how the "politics of giving and getting" is particularly salient in

2. In the Jacksonian sense, a quasi-state is simply a failed state or one that lacks internal sovereignty. This definition neglects the complex processes and consequences of globalization and self-determination movements that have created new political entities outside the traditional state system (Jackson 1990).

territories tied to self-determination and where de jure status is absent, since aid is not targeted toward a legitimate government, but rather, to nongovernmental organizations (NGOs), local actors, and preferred partners (Kolsto 2006, 723–24; Chorev 2007; King 2001, 23; Jackson 1990; Brynen 2000, 25).

External aid not only offers quasi-states opportunities for postwar reconstruction and development, but also provides the international recognition and internal sovereignty necessary for their emergence and survival. To be sure, in the pre–Gulf War period, U.S. foreign aid programs were shaped by macroeconomic and modernization theories, technical aid, the mechanics of postcolonial new nations, the politics of assisting poor countries away from communism, and dependency theories—all of which excluded unrecognized regions from directly accessing international revenues and aid-related services (Wiarda 2004; Muscat 2002, 104; Ruttan 1996, 34).[3] The international aid community that became active during this period, including the United Nations, the International Monetary Fund (IMF), and private voluntary organizations (PVOs) focused on technical assistance, large scale capital transfers, and pilot projects in strategically sovereign states. Even after U.S. bilateral assistance moved from an economic strategy of improving gross national product (GNP) to a more socially orientated program of aiding the poorest countries, the notion of state sovereignty remained sacrosanct (Ruttan 1996, 68, 94, 444). The Washington Consensus encouraged economic liberalization and institutional reform in war-torn, developing world societies; however, it offered no opportunities for unrecognized regions or quasi-states to access foreign aid directly.

The recognition of failed states, human rights abuses linked to them, and proliferation of alternative international authority structures in the 1990s created the conditions in which a "new humanitarianism" emerged (Barakat 2005, 9–10). Shaped by norms of liberal peace that aim to turn conflict-prone societies into stable ones, the new humanitarianism seeks to alter the wrongs of the past by changing regimes, compensating victims, building institutions, and reshaping political behavior. Whereas state sovereignty was previously a requirement for

---

3. Prior to this period, U.S. assistance was inflexible and shaped by self-imposed limitations on international economic assistance. For example, the U.S. Congress had rejected requests to assist the Irish famine of 1845 and Russian famine of 1881, arguing that such requests were "unconstitutional."

aid, it became a conditionality that could be transgressed by human rights issues (Hiltermann 2007, 102–3; Barakat 2005, 9–21; Mosse 2005 3–4, 13–14).

International society also became more tolerant and even supportive of marginal governments and autonomous regions, which opened new channels of assistance to otherwise isolated localities. Decolonialization processes helped further expand the narrow interpretation of self-determination to include unrecognized states and subnational movements (Bahcheli, Bartmann, and Srebrnik 2004, ix, 12–17; Chorev 2007, 6–11; King 2001; Barakat 2005, 9–21; Duffield 2001, 30; Macrae 4, 2001; Jackson 1990, 22–24, 48). Embedded in this more inclusive interpretation of aid is the commitment to protecting people through safety zones, supported by the informal UN security regime and the shared but often unclear values among the community of states of the illegality of genocide (McQueen 2005, 3–4, 20–21).[4]

Transformations in the aid regime, as well as the moral and legal framework of the state system, have been essential to creating and sustaining the Kurdish quasi-state in Iraq. Humanitarian assistance and international protection of Iraqi Kurds in the form of a safe haven and no-fly zone (UNHCR 688) helped establish a relatively secure environment that permitted international nongovernmental organizations (INGOs) to assure basic needs for local populations, resettle over two million refugees, and commence rehabilitation processes. External aid also unintentionally advanced Kurdish nationalism by offering new forms of external patronage, semi-legitimacy, and internal sovereignty to the region. During this period the Kurdish elite took advantage of international support by commencing institution-building projects and creating a Kurdistan Regional Government (KRG) in the three northern provinces of Dohuk, Arbil, and Suleymaniya.

Indeed, the evolution of the Kurdish quasi-state has not been a forward-moving process. The very nature of the early aid regime, shaped by the strategic

4. The first safety zones can be traced to the Franco-Prussian War in 1870, when Henri Dunant, founder of the Red Cross, designated certain towns in conflict areas as neutral. After various efforts by French activists for a legal codification process, the 1949 Geneva Convention and the 1977 Geneva Protocol permitted the creation of neutralized zones, which were established in the 1970s in Cyprus, Cambodia, Vietnam, Nicaragua, Argentina, Sri Lanka, and Croatia. With the end of the cold war in 1990 and the renewed commitment to maintaining international order, external aid via safety zones has expanded to protect entire civilian populations.

interests of foreign governments and international organizations, as well as regional politics, centered on checking Iraqi president Saddam Hussein and preventing the spread of weapons of mass destruction (WMD). While protecting Kurdish populations, it refused officially to recognize the KRG and had no policy agenda for the Kurdistan Region. Lacking the mandate to engage in Kurdish autonomy issues, humanitarian organizations, in turn, covered political problems with food aid (Prendergast 1996, 8). Short-term relief in the form of food and fuel handouts created mass dependency on INGOs, limited capabilities of internal governance, fed upon existing power struggles, and encouraged competition between the two main political groups, the Kurdistan Democratic Party (KDP) and the Patriotic Union of Kurdistan (PUK), for access to donor funds (Natali 1999). Within two years, the autonomous Kurdistan Region became mired in internecine party warfare, which undermined the potential benefits of the aid program as well as the region's legitimacy and internal sovereignty.

This period of conflict can easily be attributed to the positive externalities of foreign assistance. As scholars and practitioners have well argued, aid can exacerbate the root causes of insecurity, be used as an instrument of war, or be integrated into the dynamics of conflict (Prendergast 1996, 10, 17; Anderson 1999, 43–44; Jean and Rufin 1996, 15). Rent-seeking activities, corruption, and elite cleavages that impede reform also can be linked to domestic constraints such as historical legacies, weak institutions, and political culture. As in other conflict-prone, developing world societies, institutions in the Kurdistan Region are not just unstable, but chronically unstable, and often cannot absorb the advantages of aid or mechanisms of change. Kurdish elites also imposed their own strategies around aid through distribution networks, "hijacking the humanitarian infrastructure," disrupting the local economy, and diverting resources and revenues to their own advantage (Prendergast 1996, 17; Anderson 1999, 43–44).

In fact, the path-dependent nature of institutional constraints reveals that some countries or regions may be resistant to development because of entrenched interests of certain socioeconomic groups (Hout 2004, 594; Page and Van Gelder 2001; Rondinelli 1987, 3; Bratton and van de Walle 1997, 21; Ruttan 1996, 1–8). Robust authoritarianism in the Middle East, for instance, alongside traditional institutions and Islamic principles regulating contractual relationships, has resulted in a governance gap and failure to engage in real political reform or the transition to democracy (MacLean 2004; Bratton and van de Walle 1997, 32;

Schlumberger 2006, 35–37; Entelis 2005, 540; Hudson 1994, 5–8; Kuran 2004, 74–75). African countries also have resisted development, despite decades of generous levels of international humanitarian aid (Larrain-Rios 2005, 86–87, 112–13; Inglehart, 1997, 19; Brown 2003, 141–42; Roberts and Hite 2000, 18; Way 2004; Barakat 2005, 10; Ball 1996, 18; Jean 1996, 544, 578–79; Anderson 1999, 43–44; Prendergast 1996, 8).

Yet if humanitarian aid fuels predation, is constrained by certain political cultures, and can hinder development in institutionally weak societies, then what explains the transition toward stability, partial democratic norms, and economic development in the Kurdistan Region after 1996, when aid-related revenues more than tripled during the Oil for Food Programme (OFFP) administered by the United Nations from March 1996 to November 2003 under the framework of UNSCR 986? In fact, the very "warlords" that used military means and aid revenues at their disposal chose to pursue peace and political negotiation, even when their individual profit margins from the conflict remained large.

Whereas external aid can negatively impact conflict and constrain development, it can also, in an open political context with positive incentives toward willing aid recipients and necessary monitoring, encourage stability, spur economic growth, and establish long-term relationships between foreign governments and nonstate actors (Brynen 2000, 19; Anderson 1999, 34–44; Gounder 2002). With the commencement of the OFFP in 1996, the nature of external aid to the Kurdistan Region of Iraq slightly changed, which resulted in an increase in funds available for rehabilitation and new sources of income generation. In contrast to the first relief period, external aid included political engagements from foreign governments to help reconcile the feuding Kurdish elite and create an Iraqi opposition movement. Even after the abortive uprising against Saddam Hussein in 1995 and withdrawal of coalition forces and most INGOs from the region, ongoing foreign aid to Iraqi Kurds provided an environment of recognition, semi-legitimacy, and relative stability.

The Anglo-American intervention in Iraq and overthrow of Saddam Hussein in 2003 commenced yet another phase of external aid that has reshaped the development trajectory of the Kurdish quasi-state. Tied to the larger objective of stabilizing the region, engaging in the "war on terror," and securing Iraqi petroleum reserves and lucrative business revenues, the U.S.-led reconstruction project has supported long-term development and democratic principles throughout

Iraq (Carapico 2002, 379; Looney 2003a, 570–71; Alkadiri and Mohamedi 2003, 21). The creation of a federal Iraqi state, even in its imperfect form, also has enhanced the international legitimacy and internal sovereignty of the Kurdish quasi-state. In contrast to the earlier aid periods, whereby the KRG remained an unrecognized entity, after 2003 it has become an official component of the Iraqi political system, assuming its own budget, regional powers, and security responsibilities. The KRG now welcomes foreign consulates and delegations to the region and has expanded diplomatic engagements abroad. It has initiated and supported multi-million-dollar investment projects, including the exportation of petroleum in the region, while advancing reforms in the education and health care sectors. Over time, development differentials emerged so that the Kurdish north has become more viable than parts of southern and central Iraq, reinforcing the notion of a Kurdistan Region apart from the Iraqi state.

The Benefits and Constraints of Stalemate

If external aid has helped legitimize and develop the Kurdish quasi-state, why then has the KRG made no serious attempt to assert independence from the weak Iraqi state? Its economy is relatively better than that of the central government in Baghdad, its political conditions are relatively stable, and the majority of its populations have no real attachment to Iraq. The referendum conducted in the immediate post-Saddam period indicated that the vast majority of Kurds would rather be an independent entity than remain part of the Iraqi state. Instability in the central and southern parts of the country and a centralizing tendency in Baghdad also have made the interest in cooperating with the Iraqi government even less appealing to the KRG. Yet since 2003 the Kurdish elites have made important compromises in their nationalist project and have attempted to work with the central government in a federal Iraq. Instead of independence they have settled for political limbo.

Certainly, the Kurds' decision to remain part of the Iraqi state is less a function of their own political will than the constraints of the sovereignty regime and the geopolitical circumstances of the Kurdistan Region. Since the late imperial period, Kurdish nationalists have been harshly repressed for resisting the central government or for seeking political autonomy: Shaykh Mahmoud Barzinji in the 1920s, Mullah Mustafa Barzani in the 1940s, the KDP throughout the 1960s, and the PUK and KDP thereafter. The very notion of a stable, autonomous Kurdistan Region continues to irritate the central government and regional states with Kurdish populations of their own to manage. Post–Gulf War Iraqi Kurdistan also has become a magnet for cross-border Kurdish nationalist groups and the target of ongoing military incursions by regional government forces.

But if the political behavior of the Kurdish quasi-state is based largely on the nationalist will and fear of political-military reprisals, the KRG could have joined forces with the Kurdish nationalist groups, the Partîye Karkâren Kurdistane (PKK) and Pejak, an Iranian-Kurdish dissident group, based in the Qandil Mountains and border areas of their northern enclave, to challenge Iraqi forces or regional states. Such an alliance could have strengthened the military capabilities and possibly increased the legitimacy of the KRG among local populations, many of whom criticize its officials and the political parties for having "sold out" Kurdish nationalism. In fact, some Iraqi Kurds, particularly the young, believe that the only "pure" nationalists left can be found in the PKK, who continue to struggle for the Kurdish cause instead of living luxurious lives in the cities.

This option may appeal to some Kurdish nationalists; however, it disregards the political and economic realities of quasi-state existence. That is, alongside nationalist sentiment and historical legacies, the particular logic of quasi-states requires the continuation of the status quo for their survival (Kolsto 2006, 724; King 2001, 538). Quasi-states depend upon ongoing external patronage and international support to champion their cause as victims of dictatorship and human rights abuses, which, in turn, assures some form of political recognition and internal sovereignty. Most revenues are not gained from official taxation policies but rather from the central government, international donors, underground economies, and resource exploitation. These "benefits of stalemate"—recognition, legitimacy, and development derived from international aid—and the need to thrive on something else, create incentives and demands to remain connected, even in discrete ways, to the central state (Jackson 1990; Kolsto 2006, 724; King 2001, 538; Bahcheli, Bartmann, and Srebrnik 2004, 25).

Indeed, political stalemate, or incomplete international recognition, can vary according to the strategic interests of foreign governments and create different conditions and capabilities for quasi-states over time. Whereas the Palestinian quasi-state gained access to international financial institutions and representation at the United Nations, despite the failed Oslo peace process, and Kosovo recently declared independence with tacit support from the United States and its NATO allies, the Kurdish quasi-state has been tied to the ongoing international commitment to Iraqi sovereignty. Even after the overthrow of Saddam Hussein, the very nature of the external aid program has assured that the Kurdistan Region will remain part of a federal Iraq. Political stalemate has been reinforced by the refusal or inability of Iraqi and Kurdish elites to compromise on particular status issues, such as power sharing and boundary issues, particularly Kirkuk and the disputed territories (article 140 of the Iraqi constitution) (Chorev 2007, 13; Kolsto 2006, 723; King 2001).[5]

Stalemate can be further encouraged by a policy of maintaining the status quo, which can negatively affect development by restricting the type of aid that quasi-states can solicit and receive. For instance, although the KRG receives its own budget to administer the region autonomously, it still has no legal right to secure international loans or borrow at concessional rates to encourage long-term capital investment. Foreign investors also are generally wary of doing business in quasi-state environments in which contracts are not legally binding (Kolsto 2006, 729). The KRG may have arranged direct petroleum drilling ventures with numerous foreign companies; however, the vast majority of large international firms refuse to conduct business in Arbil, despite the relative calm and potential for growth. Nor is the KRG permitted to create an independent army, establish foreign policy, or develop natural resources without consultation and potential tensions with the central government, no matter how weak this government may be. Political stalemate in the oil-rich province of Kirkuk has further disadvantaged the KRG, where the economic payoffs of territorial accession for the Kurdistan Region are high.[6] The benefits of implementing article 140 of the Iraqi

5. Kirkuk was one of the *sanjaqs* of the Ottoman Empire in the Sharezur and Mosul *vilayets*, and in 1919 became an independent province. After five years of autonomy Kirkuk, as well as other *liwas* of Kurdistan (Suleymaniya, Arbil, and Mosul), were annexed to Iraq in 1925 as part of a larger Mosul province. Administrative units within Kirkuk also changed, decreasing from eight districts (*qadha*) to four by 1947.

6. Numerous studies on post–Gulf War Iraq, including the World Food Programme Survey (WFP 2004) and UNICEF's 1999 household survey, focus on the sanctions regime in the southern and central regions, making conclusions without including the Kurdish governorates (Alnasrawi

constitution would expand the territorial boundaries of Kurdistan and help build a self-sustaining Kurdistan economy.

Still, given the logic of quasi-state survival, the Kurdistan Region has much to gain by maintaining the status quo. Stalemate can advantage the Kurdish quasi-state economy, which is often better than the failed central state of which it is still a part, by producing positive externalities for its perpetrators that include wealth generation and customs revenues from legal and illicit trading (King 2001, 538–45). For the KRG the benefits of stalemate include 17 percent of the budget from Baghdad, or about US$6 billion in 2009; multi-billion-dollar investment projects; and lucrative commercial activities with neighboring states, namely Turkey, Iran, and more recently, regional Arab countries. Moreover, stalemate offers continued external patronage and international recognition, no matter how limited it may be, which provides the opportunity structures to expand the administrative and political capabilities of the KRG inside Iraq over time.

The problematic, therefore, is not whether aid positively or negatively influences development, but the extent to which it offers new forms of internal sovereignty and leverage to quasi-state entities and the impact this leverage may have on relations with the parent state. Even when quasi-states or subnational units gain access to humanitarian resources, this assistance must be evaluated in relation to other units within the state, and in particular, the central government. Changes in distribution modalities and support mechanisms, alongside the enhanced autonomy of subnational units, can encourage struggles over resources and political power (Suhrke and Strand 2005, 146–52). For instance, if the central government subsidizes fuel and food for local populations and suddenly withdraws this support, regional administrations come under increasing pressure to fill the void, which can exacerbate tensions with central authorities and between regions for revenues. Similarly, aid revenues reallocated from the Kurdistan Region to other parts of Iraq can encourage new competitions with Baghdad over access to donor and investor funds.

2001; Gazdar and Hussain 2002). The few studies on the Kurdistan Region conflate the aid program into one period and are overly focused on the predatory behavior of the local elite, assuming that patronage is based on domination and nonbeneficial to society as a whole (Graham-Brown 2002, 283; Barnett, Eggleston, and Webber 2003; Leezenberg 2003; Bozarslan 1996).

Distinct historical legacies also matter because they shape the attitudes of quasi-states toward the central government before aid programs commence. Whereas the quasi-states that emerged from the former Soviet Union had a legacy of central government support, the Kurdish quasi-state emerged from the dictatorial Ba'athist regime and hostile regional governments, which were hardly templates to be replicated in the region (King 2001). No Kurd would insist, as Abkhazians or South Ossetians have of their Russian patrons, of maintaining Iraqi, Turkish, or Iranian bases on Kurdish territory. Instead, the KRG has requested permanent U.S. forces in the region to help guarantee long-term protection against the central government.

External aid to quasi-states can reinforce historical legacies by creating new forms of competition with the central government over political legitimacy. For instance, in Iraq the legacy of a strong central government, breakdown of power in Baghdad, and development of autonomous regional entities after 2003 have aggravated tensions over revenues, petroleum rights, and territorial boundary claims, particularly in Kirkuk. The lingering sense of distrust, if not fear, by Kurdish communities of the central government has created important obstacles to establishing ongoing, positive relations between Arbil and Baghdad based on power-sharing.

Even then, the Kurdish quasi-state's heightened antagonisms with the central government must be examined alongside pressing demands for external legitimacy, greater internal sovereignty, and economic growth and development. Liberalization processes tied to the aid program in post-Saddam Iraq have created new interdependences between the Kurdistan Region, neighboring states, and the central government. Kurds have gained large representation in the Iraqi central government and have established important administrative and political linkages with Baghdad. These linkages have maintained or developed ties to Arab communities, and even strengthened them in some areas. Populations from the south travel to, and temporarily work in, the Kurdistan Region, where employment opportunities and secure living conditions are available. In this increasingly complex socioeconomic and political order, the lines between development, economic opportunism, and Kurdish nationalism have become increasingly blurred.

The argument that aid-induced development can reshape Kurdish-state relations will be examined in five chapters analyzing the political economy of the

Kurdistan Region from the early state period to the present. Chapter 1 will examine the prewar conditions in which historical legacies and structural impediments to development were institutionalized. Chapters 2 through 5 will examine the different post–Gulf War aid programs and their influences on the evolution of the Kurdish quasi-state. External aid programs will be disaggregated into three phases: (1) emergency relief phase (1991–96); (2) OFFP phase (1996–2003); and (3) democracy mission phase (2003–present). Although aid programs are not mutually exclusive, these categorizations are used because they represent a significant change in the nature of aid from the previous period. Evolution over time can help determine relationships that may exist between the nature of aid, types of institutions, sectoral disbursements across regions, and variations in Kurdish-state relations during each period (Jean and Rufin 1996, 13).

During each phase, certain questions will be addressed: According to what strategic interests, norms, and objectives are aid programs designed and resources allocated to different institutions and groups? How significant are international resources in financing rehabilitation and development, and to what extent do these finances contribute to shaping the aid program? How has aid affected the distribution of power at local, regional, and national levels, including issues of equity and national identity? How has aid helped develop or disrupt local norms and political culture that encourage participation? What types of political strategies have local elites imposed around aid? Which groups benefited and which were disadvantaged from the aid programs? What types of informal economies, income generation, and patronage have been reinforced, weakened, or newly established? To what extent has aid-related development contributed to the daily lives of local populations?

External aid will be measured by the purpose for which official humanitarian and development assistance is designed and the manner in which it is distributed. It can include disaster relief; development and reconstruction assistance; and security, financial, and political support that creates different opportunities or constraints for stability and growth (Duarte 2003, 4–5; Brynen 2000, 25; Billet 1993, 5).[7] Security assistance can provide a necessary environment in which

---

7. Aid can be distributed as official development assistance (ODA), including multilateral or bilateral assistance, foreign direct investment and external debt, or donations, which include grants, loans, or a combination of the two.

rehabilitation can occur, but it can also encourage instability by undermining civilian leaders and antagonizing radical groups (Barakat and Chard 2005, 173–74). Conditionalities, timing, and amount of aid also matter. Donor agencies may impose criteria on aid recipient groups in the attempt to alter or encourage certain types of development or political behavior. Timing includes the commencement and duration of each component of the aid program. Amount refers to the total donor and INGO spending in each region as a percentage of total aid. Some programs can be generous in financing but limited in time, which can prevent the consolidation of local capacity-building processes.

Development refers to general processes of economic recovery, political reform, and social change that encourage participation, strengthen stability, reduce the vulnerability of populations to sickness and economic malaise, and increase the capacity of institutions to respond to local needs, such as the enforcement of law and provision of public goods and services.[8] It can include modernization processes such as industrialization, urbanization, secularization, education, bureaucratization, and mass production (Ingelhart 1997, 69–73). Indicators include economic structure, property rights, levels and distribution of income, type of political institutions, role of community-based organizations, individual liberties, quality of education and social capital, the status of women, and attitudinal changes, including the movement away from traditional-religious norms to rational-legal ones based on merit (Calvert and Calvert 2007, 3–4; Wiarda 2004, 3, 45; Brown 2003; Brynen 2000, 7–9; 312–13; Barakat 2005, 10; Page and van Gelder 2001, 17, 23; Reilly and Phillpot 2002, 913–26; Fukayama 2002; Krishna 2002, 58–62; Dube 1988, 2).

Development processes also will be examined as they affect the internal sovereignty of the Kurdish quasi-state over time. Different degrees of external recognition tied to aid create varying opportunities for quasi-state development, which in turn can affect leverage, levels of internal capabilities, and forms of local governance. Low levels of external recognition are likely to stunt development

---

8. Although development is often used interchangeably with democratization and modernization, this approach is misleading and lends itself to an inaccurate interpretation of political transformations in regions that have no real understanding or political will to democratize. Additionally, given the absence of reliable statistics or quantitative data in the region, development measurements cannot include traditional indicators such as GNP, trade figures, or employment levels.

and internal sovereignty, whereby higher levels of recognition can encourage greater internal sovereignty and political institution building. Even then, development processes and the leverage they accord to quasi-states can be impeded by domestic constraints, such as political culture, historical legacies, and institutional weakness.

The effects of development processes on Kurdistan-state relations will be measured by formal and informal mechanisms as they relate to (1) economic and commercial relations; (2) Kurdish political demands for autonomy, including the status of Kirkuk; and (3) cultural and social ties. Linkages can include resource, revenue, and power sharing, educational exchanges and interactions between local populations that bring Kurds and the rest of Iraqis together or apart on a daily basis. While economic and cultural linkages can be compromising, political relations over Kurdish autonomy can be hostile or unchanging, indicating that factors other than external aid may be at work in shaping Kurdish-state relations, and the possibilities of negotiating Kurdish autonomy inside the territorial boundaries of Iraq. These linkages can give greater insight into the patterns of behavior between the quasi-state and central government under different levels of economic development.

By examining the evolution of the Kurdish quasi-state as a function of foreign aid policies and programs over time, this detailed comparative study challenges criticisms of external interventions in underdeveloped, conflict-prone regions as necessarily destabilizing or ineffective. Rather, it suggests that for quasi-states or unrecognized regions in failed states, external aid can be a necessary and vital force in mitigating conflict, encouraging self-sustainability, and advancing peace. More specifically, this case study challenges the claim that foreign intervention in Iraq was needless and without positive consequences. For the Kurdistan Region, foreign aid programs have encouraged important development processes and economic interdependencies with regional states and Baghdad. These relationships, and their consequent transformations in the political economy, have established the conditions in which political cooperation has become increasingly possible, if not vital, for the long-term survivability of the Kurdish quasi-state in Iraq.

THE KURDISH QUASI-STATE

1

Structural Legacies

DURING THE COLONIAL AND POSTCOLONIAL PERIODS IN IRAQ, external aid to the Kurdistan Region was virtually nonexistent. The strategic interests of competing foreign governments were based on defining territorial borders, stabilizing the new Iraqi state, and securing petroleum resources. Even with the emergence of the state petroleum industry in the early 1950s, the nature of foreign aid focused on technical assistance, capital investments, and financial inputs to the sovereign Iraqi state and not the unrecognized Kurdistan Region. Economic isolation and underdevelopment was exacerbated by state authoritarianism in an increasingly ethnicized and repressive political context. In the absence of international recognition, external patronage, or internal sovereignty, the Kurdistan Region had no leverage, incentives, or institutional capabilities to sustain positive ties with the central government. The relationship that emerged was based on patronage, dependency, and open conflict.

Aidless and Agrarian

As in most postconflict situations, World War I (1914–18) left the Kurdistan provinces of the Ottoman Empire in economic and political havoc. Mass refugee populations created ethnic and religious imbalances in sensitive border areas, disrupted markets led to food shortages, and depleted resources left populations without basic services. Missionary groups backed by European governments provided local assistance; however, their efforts focused on select Christian communities in the Turkish provinces and not the Muslim, Kurdish tribal regions of Iraq. Even after the Ottoman Empire disintegrated and the Kurdistan Region became a battlefield between nationalists, religious leaders, and foreign governments, local populations had no access to humanitarian aid that could have provided shelter, emergency relief, and rehabilitation to the region. U.S. President Woodrow Wilson's Fourteen Point program offered the ideological impetus for protecting minority group rights, particularly for the Kurds. Still, the institutional framework and international support for foreign aid transfers to the unrecognized Kurdistan Region were unavailable. Certain Kurdish leaders received political promises from colonial officers, yet this assistance had no official financial backing or legal mechanisms of enforcement. It also terminated when the British assumed control of Mosul province and the Kurds lost their bid for statehood in 1923.

To be sure, the British-mandated government welcomed foreign aid as part of its larger strategic objective to develop and industrialize Iraq, which included securing Iraqi petroleum concessions.[1] With the advice of international technical consultants and in coordination with the British Middle East Office (BMEO), it passed a series of laws to stimulate agricultural markets and industrial growth. The 1926 law for the encouragement of cultivators to use pumps, the 1929 law for the encouragement of industry, and the 1933 law for customs tariffs canceled certain customs duties for imported capital goods, imposed high tariffs on consumption items, and encouraged private investment. The new Iraqi state subsidized grain exports, imported machinery, and distributed seeds to farmers (Dahiri 1976, 87; Langley 1961, 70; Haj 1997 48). To boost the tobacco industry, the main cash crop of Iraq grown in the Kurdistan Region, the government passed a law to support tobacco production, established a tobacco monopoly in 1939 that fixed prices, supported farmers' incomes, and increased customs duties on imported tobacco. The central government also invested in infrastructure projects to expand commercial relations between the Kurdistan Region and Baghdad. It spent about 3 million Iraqi dinars (OID) building a railway from Kirkuk to Arbil so that by 1950 the Kurdish north was linked to the south and traded goods were transported from Mosul to Basra and Baghdad (Langley 1961, 117).[2]

1. The Iraqi oil industry was initially based on a system of concession agreements between the central government and oil companies, which commenced in the late nineteenth century. The foreign oil companies, or concessioners, had the sole right to develop and export the petroleum and to determine output and prices (Alnasrawi 1994, 1–2).

2. Until 1931 the Iraqi economy was tied to the British sterling, although as a member of the Indian monetary areas, Indian rupees were used as an official means of exchange. They were then replaced with the Iraq dinar (Iversen 1954, 5).

As the granary of Iraq and main food producer of the country, the largely rain-fed Kurdistan Region, with 1.4 million hectares of arable land, had much to gain from the state's agrarian support policies. Central government control of market structures created a situation in which the agriculturally rich Kurdistan Region supplied a large proportion of the country's internal food needs and exports to Europe. From the late nineteenth century until the mid-1930s Iraq exported about 100,000 metric tons (MT) of grain annually, the majority of which was produced in the Kurdistan Region (Kirk and Sawdon 2002, iii–iv; Dahiri 1976, 280; Issawi 1966, 133; Langley 1961, 25, 70).[3] The expansion of trade during World War II, despite high export and import taxes, and harvest failures in 1948 and 1949, further stimulated agricultural production and animal husbandry. By the early 1950s grain production in the Kurdistan Region increased by 56 percent, and constituted about 70 percent of the country's total wheat production and about 43 percent of the country's exports other than oil (Haj 1997, 6; IBRD 1952, 145). Agriculture also was the most important source of state tax, providing 29 percent of the national income and employing four-fifths of the Iraqi labor force (Ahmad 2002 17; Haj 1997, 35; Issawi 1966, 187; Haseeb 1963, 17; Langley 1961, 91). Further, the fertile Kurdistan Region sourced water from the Euphrates and Tigris rivers, which was needed for irrigated crops in southern and central Iraq.

Despite these economic support structures, the Kurdistan Region remained one of the most isolated, underdeveloped, and unstable parts the country. During the colonial period Kurdish nationalist and tribal groups led by Shaykh Mahmoud Barzinji, Shaykh Ahmad of Barzan, and Mullah Mustafa Barzani revolted against the central government; Christian and Muslim communities clashed in the Badinan region; Kurdish *aghas* were engaged in land and tribal disputes; and urbanizing communities demonstrated in the streets against labor laws, food prices, and lack of services in the city centers (Tripp 2007, 72). In 1946 some Kurds created the Kurdistan Democratic Party (KDP) to advance Kurdish nationalist

---

3. The Kurdistan Region can be further divided into food economy areas, such as the rain-fed plains, the mountainous zones, and the semiarid steppe. The rain-fed areas include the Arbil, Akra, and Harir plains and the area west of Dohuk. The mountainous zone includes regions near the Turkish and Iranian border, and the semiarid steppe includes Dashti Koya in southern Arbil and Germian.

1. Kurdish demonstrations in Baghdad, ca. 1948. The sign says, "Kurdish groups appeal for the releasing of Barzinji's citizens, and providing food, clothes, and shelter for the families." Photograph courtesy of Rafiq Studio, Suleymaniya.

claims and support cross-border Kurdish communities, including the short-lived Mahabad Republic in Iran. These activities reinforced the volatile relationship between the Kurdistan Region and Baghdad, as well as between Kurdish groups. What explains these conflictual relations, particularly among the populations that had the most to benefit from the Iraqi agrarian economy?

The nature of external aid offered neither international recognition nor internal sovereignty to the rural Kurdistan Region, which allowed isolation, instability, and underdevelopment to prevail. Despite appeals by Kurds and other minority groups, such as Assyrians, Ezidis, and Turcomans, for international protection, the League of Nations and the British government made no real effort to guarantee minority rights in Iraq (Tripp 2007, 72). The 1925 Constitution of the Kingdom of Iraq mentioned the "Rights of the People," and assured that "no differentiations" would be made according to language, race, or creed and that all individuals would have freedom of expression, liberty of association, and rights of ownership (articles 6–12). Still, the issue of "rights" was discussed in a general sense and without reference to any particular ethnic, religious, or linguistic group

(1925 Constitution of Iraq). Rather, British colonial officers assured Iraq's membership in the League of Nations, which after 1932 guaranteed its independence and sovereignty as well as Britain's interests in the state. To this end, the BMEO and central government focused on protecting Iraqi trade routes with India and securing shares in the petroleum market, which Britain controlled until 1972.

Petrolizing and industrializing Iraq led to a certain type of development strategy that favored Baghdad and its environs. The Kurdish north may have had a key role in the Iraqi agrarian economy; however, it was not part of development processes that could have created more complex socioeconomic and political structures to integrate the outlying regions with the central government. The capacity link also was weak, with minimal inputs of capital, labor, raw materials, or technology coming to or being produced in the Kurdistan Region (Bookman 1991, 155). Although water pumps increased from 21 to 2,400 in 1929–30, 60 percent were installed in Baghdad province. Half of the 320 combines and 50 tractors distributed in Iraq were concentrated in Mosul and Baghdad (IBRD 1952). Of the 1,450 large-scale establishments and 30,000 small-scale businesses that employed 250,000 people in Iraq, only a small handful were located in the Kurdistan Region. Whereas Basra, Baghdad, Amara, and Hilla received pumping and electrical power stations that provided water to more than half of the existing municipalities, the Kurdistan Region had the lowest in the country. About 90 percent of electrical power was consumed in the urban centers of Baghdad, Kirkuk, Basra, and Mosul (IBRD 1952, 61; Langley 1961, 131).[4] Similarly, the 1956 distribution of national income had large disparities among the provinces, with the highest contribution from Baghdad (29.7 percent), Kirkuk (15.4 percent), and Basra (11.5 percent). After removing oil revenues, Kirkuk's contribution was only about 6 percent, while Baghdad's increased to 36 percent, and Mosul's was about 11 percent (Haseeb 1964, 28–29).

Certainly, differentiated regional development patterns commenced prior to the colonial period. Migration patterns led to variations in urbanization processes across regions. The settling of nomadic groups across Iraq from the late nineteenth to mid–twentieth century declined at a larger rate in the southern

---

4. For example, in 1953 the amount of installed kilowatts (KW) in power-generating facilities in Arbil and Suleymaniya was about 1,500 KW for municipal plants and 655 KW for industrial plants and railways. In Baghdad it was about 42,000 KW and 11,000 KW respectively.

2. Flood in Arbil city, ca. 1936. Photograph courtesy of Qala Antique, Arbil.

and central regions than in the Kurdish north. Although the rise of towns and trading activities more than tripled in the northern region, rural communities remained almost double the urban percentage, with 59 percent in the countryside and 36 percent in cities. Population shifts encouraged the transformation of economic activities from caravan trading to agriculture and, later, tertiary activities such as trade, public services, and transportation, most of which centered in Baghdad (Issawi 1966, 157–59). During the late Ottoman Empire, Baghdad city and its environs represented about 42 percent of all occupations, while the northern regions, including Mosul and Kirkuk, represented 28 percent (Issawi 1966, 160). Baghdad was an important point of the caravan trade between the Mediterranean and the Persian Gulf and Iran and developed trade relations with the British and foreign companies.

The main regions where opportunities for capital and industrial development were available were the cities of Baghdad, Basra, and Mosul, and in the sectors that supplied consumer goods, such as construction items, cigarettes, textiles, food, and cooking oil. In contrast, the Kurdistan Region had no economic infrastructure, export market, airport, port, or wealth to develop an autonomous

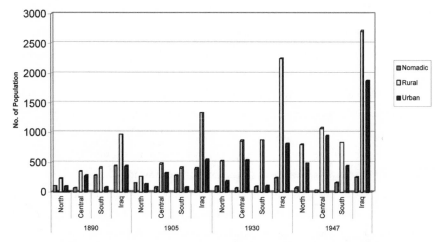

3. Changes in the nomadic-urban composition of the Iraqi population, 1890–1947. *Source:* Issawi (1966, 157–61). Note: the northern region of Mosul includes the *liwas* of Arbil, Kirkuk, Mosul, and Suleymaniya. The central region includes *liwas* of Baghdad, Diyala, Dulaim, Hilla, Karbala, and Kut. The southern region (former Basra *vilayet*) includes *liwas* of Amarah, Basra, Diwaniya, and Mutafiq. In 1890 Hilla included Diwaniya, which was moved from the central region.

commercial economy. By 1912 the local economy of Suleymaniya consisted of 1,155 shops, 70 tea houses, gun makers, and one small soap factory that produced 500 tons of soap annually (Şwani 2002, 47–48). Only a small number of people were engaged in business, and even then there was no Kurdish merchant class. Wealthy business and commercial communities comprised Christians from Mosul and Jews from Suleymaniya and Dohuk, and not the majority Kurdish Muslim populations.

Still, patterns set during the colonial and postcolonial periods created the preconditions for differentiated regional development in Iraq (Larrain Rios 2005, 86–87; Sinha 2003, 463). The particular nature of early Iraqi development affected the distribution of power at the national, regional, and local levels by reinforcing variations in sectoral and regional capacities. Instead of creating village councils or a system of institutional governance in the Kurdistan Region that could have encouraged participation, the British employed the cost-effective policy of indirect rule. This governance strategy supported tribal shaykhs in different localities and allowed the localized and fragmented system of tribal rule to continue within the closed Iraqi political system. Tribes were given particular privileges over urban communities, including tax benefits, relative autonomy in their region, and direct access to central government officers (Natali 2005; Batatu 1979). The absence of external aid also prevented the economic recovery necessary for political reform and changing social attitudes in the Kurdistan Region. For instance, although Suleymaniya city opened its first hospital in 1911–12, the majority of health facilities were located in school buildings. Some British physicians were available; however, local populations depended upon folkloric remedies and not scientific treatment or medical advice (Şwani 2002, 69–72).

State control of the infrastructure and productivity further prevented the Kurdistan Region from accessing merchant capital that could have encouraged entrepreneurship, private markets, and economic growth. Even though the Kurdish north was situated inside the important trade route with Iran, Europe, Turkey, Mosul, and Baghdad, it served as a transit zone and had no important part of production processes. The Arbil-Basra railroad stopped functioning in 1950 because of insufficient state funds and private investment capital. High transaction costs and noncomplex economic organization based on personal exchanges without third-party enforcement further limited the advantages of official trade in the Kurdistan Region (Hout 2004, 594).

Indeed, even if foreign aid was available and state-generated revenues were equally distributed to the Kurdistan Region, local political conditions, institutional weakness, and structural constraints would have hindered development processes. From the early colonial period to the eve of the Iraqi revolution, the central government was in a continuous state of flux, with numerous coups d'état and social unrest (Tripp 2007, 75–104). The persistence of the British presence in Iraq, the financial crisis and food shortages in 1947, and the growing anticolonial movement added to the political instability of the post–World War II period. The Palestinian War had its own repercussions on Iraqi politics and society, most notably with the declaration of martial law in 1948, eventual exodus of the Jewish community, court martials, and emergent pan-Arab nationalism (Tripp 2007, 115–20).

In this unstable context, government capacity was weak, credit facilities were unavailable, farmland was barely mechanized, and storage was inadequate. Farmers either had to borrow from private individuals at excessive interest rates or from the state agricultural bank, which had insufficient reserves (IBRD 1952,

29). By 1950 the central government did not even have a separate ministry of agriculture, despite the leading role of the agricultural sector in the Iraqi economy. The legal system, grounded in Islamic law and traditional institutions, created no advantages for a merchant class linked to capital accumulation. Despite changes in the Law for the Encouragement of Industry in 1950, which included exemptions from income taxes and customs duties and rent-free land for ten years, the sociopolitical and economic climate was unsupportive of industrial development (IBRD 1952, 40). Two-thirds of the population still lived in rural areas, with about 550,000 people in Baghdad municipality and another 300,000 in Mosul and Kirkuk. The remaining 350,000 lived in towns of over 15,000 people, with smaller areas of districts (*qadha*) and subdistricts (*nahiyya*) essentially as villages (IBRD 1952, 127). High levels of illiteracy, absence of skilled manpower and technical expertise, and risk-averse landowners made even the noblest efforts of reform insurmountable (Kuran 2004, 78–87).

The rural Kurdistan Region also was tied to segmented social structures unsupportive of change (Marr 1985, 137). Endogamous family ties and close relationships between family, work, and territory formed the basis of an informal bazaar economy, whereby the major livelihood was agrarian-based subsistence farming that focused on domestic markets. Authority structures centered on personal contacts and not merit, bureaucracy, or elected officials, which resulted in a hierarchy of individual personalities that defined social and political organizations (Barth 1953, 50, 79). There was no official court system but tribal chiefs who acted as arbitrators of tribal law (Hay 1921, 68-69). Ascriptive forms of identity and vertical networks created an important form of social cleavage and bonding functions for Kurdish society. Yet they impeded the development of positive social capital needed for trust and cooperation outside the family unit or more complex associations in which decision making could be diffused at the local levels (Reilly and Phillpot 2002, 906–7).[5]

5. Social capital refers to features of social organization such as networks, norms, and social trust that facilitate coordination and cooperation for mutual benefit. It can encourage information sharing, collective action, and decision making. Social capital can also have negative effects. Rent-seeking organizations that provide goods and services, such as the Mafia, can emerge in the attempt to control free riding (Collier 2002, 34; Grootaert and van Bastelaer 2002, 3).

4. Arbil bazaar, late Monarchy period. Photograph courtesy of Alwan Antique, Arbil.

Traditional power structures shaped the nature of land tenure relations and prevented a system of enforced property rights, an important prerequisite for sustained economic development. About 80 percent of Iraqi land was *miri,* or state owned, and 20 percent was *tapu,* or cultivated individually. According to the *miri* system, the state leased land to cultivators by annual contracts based on a crop-sharing system. The government owned the land, while farmers had the right to cultivate it and keep production, which ranged from 20 to 50 percent of the receipts from sales (Issawi 1966, 163–64; Hay 1921, 68). The *tapu* system of land tenure established under the Ottoman administration was not based on systematic grants, but rather on one that support privileged groups. Even after the Ottoman legal code altered land tenure relations and created some free-holding lands, large tracts of land continued to be registered in family names (Issawi 1966, 164; Barth 1953, 53; IBRD 1952, 137–38). In the absence of systematic land administration and efficient, individual property rights, the landlord state had the right to arbitrarily issue contracts and collect taxes on the land, leaving cultivators without protection (North 1990, 51–53).

To be sure, the Iraqi central government passed land codes that prevented communal ownership and legalized the notion of property rights.[6] It introduced *lasmah* tenure through the 1932 cadastral survey, recognized prescriptive rights to tribal territories, and accepted the demise of the *iqta* system (IBRD 1952, 138–40). However, British colonial policies tolerated tribal customary law, allowing land tenure to be shaped by tribal power. In the Kurdish region of Balik in Rowanduz province, for example, about 90 percent of the land in each village belonged to the *agha,* who negotiated grazing rights, water usage with neighboring villages, and general assistance to the villagers (Gerdi 2005, 34–47).[7] Even with increasing penetration of the state administration into the governorates over time, the role of the *agha*s in the daily social, economic, and political life of the villages did not weaken. Rather, it became linked to Baghdad via provincial governors, who tolerated the *agha*s' power and co-opted the tribes as a means of maintaining order in the outlying regions.

This is why the expansion of agricultural production and grain exports did not necessarily lead to a rise in crop yields, economic development, or wealth across the Kurdistan Region. The concentration of cultivable land holdings—55 percent of which was controlled by 1 percent of the landowners—created a simple class hierarchy of landowners, tenant farmers, and intermediary capitalists in which the crop was unevenly divided (Haj 1997, 4, 10–19, 32; Safa 1982, 7; Barth 1953, 22–24, 133; Issawi 1966, 15, 133, 170–76; Dahiri 1976, 71, 92–104; Hasan 1970, 351; Costello 1977, 47; Batatu 1979, 148). In the Kurdistan Region, the *agha* established a system of subcontracting out parts of the land to an intermediary

6. Interview with Mr. Singar and family members in Mirakan village, Arbil governorate, Apr. 8, 2006. Landholdings were generally large; only 15 percent was less than 1,000 *donum*s. Some tribal areas combined small-sized holdings for larger plots of land. In those areas where tribal ties were weak, the cultivator depended upon state contracts and smaller-sized, inefficient plots of about forty *donum*s. Property rights also varied according to the nature of the tribe, size of the estates, and crop production. Additionally, the role of the *agha* was never a homogenous one across Kurdish society but based on the nature of the land, water sources, and production outputs in the villages. In the regions where water sources are abundant (irrigation or high rainfall) and the land is flat and fertile, the *agha*s' powers are generally greater than in regions, such as Mirakan, where rainfall in minimal or where villagers engage in animal husbandry as their main source of production.

7. The three clans of Rowanduz were represented by Mullah Sherefi, Sheqdani (Shweyzuri), and Sukri Nasrawan. All claim to be the son of Mullah Shafi.

capitalist for a fixed time period, who in turn collected rent from the tenant through a portion of the crop. Where the capitalist was not available, the Kurdish *agha* received payment directly from the tenant farmer (Gerdi 2005, 33–35; Barth 1953, 133–35; Langley 1961, 51; Haj 1997, 2; Hasan 1970, 257, 350). Yet the risk-averse Kurdish *agha*-cum-tribal shaykh, now an absentee landlord and urban consumer, was unwilling to invest in long-term saving and capital projects and instead hoarded his profits or purchased land.

The dependent and closed nature of the Kurdish economy left political and commercial relationships confined to isolated localities and prone to conflict. Tribes, *aghas*, and shaykhs became the links between the Kurdistan Region and the central government and not local administrations based on bureaucratic rationality and official mechanisms of exchange. Absence of reliable transportation and communication networks, viable institutions that incorporated illiterate populations into political processes, and democratic norms of citizen rights also prevented the emergence of political organizations and participation of groups into associational life. The semi-clandestine KDP was not part of an open multi-party system that encouraged political diversity, representation, or participation in the Kurdistan Region. Rather, it served as an umbrella organization of largely tribal and some urban educated communities without revenues or authority to engage in autonomous decision making or administration.

These trends occurred alongside the emergence of an exclusionary Iraqi identity in the form of *qawmiyya* Arab nationalism and discrimination against the Kurds by successive Iraqi governments, which exacerbated the sense of isolation, resentment, and difference within the Kurdistan Region.[8] Baghdad pacified the tribal shaykhs but bombed Kurdish villages intermittently, proscribed Kurdish nationalist organizations and opposition groups, and started to Arabize Kurdish territories, including the petroleum-rich region of Kirkuk. In the early 1930s the central government sent some Arab tribes to settle in Kirkuk and gave

---

8. *Qawmiyya* Arab nationalism refers to pan-Arab nationalism. It emphasizes the revival of the Arab nation, of which Iraq was a central part, and does not recognize the authenticity of non-Arab identities. It can be contrasted to *wataniyya* nationalism, or Iraqi patriotism, which focuses on an Iraqi identity based on linguistic and cultural ties between groups living in the same geographical area. *Wataniyya* nationalism recognizes the local identities of non-Arab groups and views the Kurds as partners in Iraq. See Natali (2005, 35–36).

Arab officers positions in the Kirkuk local administration (Talabani 2004, 21). Ethnic and territorial distinctions started to emerge between Kurds and Arabs and between the Kurdistan Region and the rest of Arab Iraq.

Still, Kurdish-state relations did not center on Kurdish autonomy or Kirkuk, but rather on the borders of the new Iraqi state and its political system: how it should be modernized, the role of Islam, the relationship to the larger Arab union, and recognition of Kurdish rights and territories (Atlasi Kirkuk 2006, 9–16; Khorshid, 2005, 53; Mohammed 2005, 22–25; Talabani 2004, 9–10; Yapp 1987, 138). Representation in the Kirkuk administration, as well as in the early Iraqi government, was based on population majorities, which were not ethnicized or exclusive of ethnic communities. Outlying provinces were administered by local stakeholders and shaped by traditional norms, while intercommunal relations were based on a relatively balanced distribution of power among Kurds, Arabs, and Turcomans.[9] In Kirkuk, two-thirds of the members of the Kirkuk governorate in the Baghdad parliament were Kurds, and the other third was Turcoman (Talabani 2004, 21). By the mid-1960s, except for the al-Hadidi tribe, Arabs were still a minority in Kirkuk province and were virtually absent from the city center. Social norms also were tolerant of Kurds, Turcomans, and Arabs as part of the Sunni Muslim community. Kurdish and Arab leftists interacted as part of the urban educated communities and shared objectives of modernizing the country, supporting state socialism, and weakening the power of the tribal *aghas* and shaykhs.

Technical Aid to the Iraqi State

External aid assumed a more significant role in Iraqi development after the discovery of petroleum in the early 1950s. Numerous international lending institutions and foreign governments visited Iraq during this period, including the

---

9. Interview with Arif Qorbani, former director of the Kirkuk city television station and independent researcher, Arbil, Oct. 15, 2006. Most Arabs were transferred to the Hawija district of Kirkuk, an area known for livestock raising, and were not made part of the city power structure. In 1935, the Baghdad parliament appointed for the first time six Kirkukis to represent the province in the central government. The representation included four Kurds, one Turcoman, and one Arab from Hawija, who was officially referred to as "the representative of the desert."

International Bank for Reconstruction and Development (IBRD), the World Bank, the United Nations Development Programme (UNDP), and the Export-Import (EXIM) bank. The governments of the United Arab Emirates, Qatar, and Saudi Arabia offered credits and loans to Iraq, as well as oil supplies. Japan provided bilateral assistance in grants and loans; European governments funded exports and development, particularly in the pharmaceutical industries; and the Soviet Union helped reorganize agriculture by modernizing machines, factories, materials, and equipment (Smolansky and Smolansky 1991, 20–21; Khadduri 1978, 123).

Still, foreign aid was based on short-term consultancies, private capital flows, multilateral portfolio investments, and financial credits to the Iraqi state, mainly in the central region. It did not include humanitarian aid, minority groups' rights, civil-society building, or sustainable development programs that could have encouraged urbanization processes, weakened traditional power structures, and strengthened political institutions in the underdeveloped Kurdish north. Exogenous assistance also lacked significant involvement by the United States, whose post–World War II foreign aid policy was tied to security and political interests shaped by anticommunism, containment policy, and the Point Four Program (Ruttan 1996, 4–5, 49–53; Rondinelli 1987, 1).[10] Even during the "development decade" of the 1960s, U.S. president John F. Kennedy's new period of economic assistance to developing countries, which was marked by the creation of the U.S. Agency for International Development (USAID) and the proliferation of public foundations, private voluntary organizations (PVOs), and INGOs, U.S. foreign aid did not target the Iraqi state or its unrecognized Kurdistan Region (Ruttan 1996, 77). Rather, it was set in cold-war politics and aimed at strengthening strategically important, peripheral countries by providing military and economic assistance to Korea, China, Southeast Asia, Greece, Turkey, Europe, Latin America, and Africa. In fact, the overall percentage of

10. The Point Four Program refers to the fourth point of U.S. President Harry Truman's inaugural address of January 20, 1949. It represents a shift in U.S. foreign aid policy focusing on the root causes of underdevelopment by transferring U.S. scientific and technical knowledge to encourage growth. U.S. support for the strategic purposes of aid has been channeled into the Economic Support Fund (ESF). From the early 1960s to the mid-1970s, South Vietnam received about 90 percent of the funds. South Korea and Taiwan were also important ESF recipients.

U.S. aid to the Middle East in general and Iraq in particular was relatively small. Of the nearly US$8 billion allocated to the Middle East in 1950–70, only $95 million in loans and grants was targeted to Iraq, with $45 million for economic development and $50 million for military expenditures (Sharp 2005, 2; Alnasrawi 1994, 29; Ruttan 1996, 279).

Indeed, early republican Iraq was ill-prepared to receive external aid. The bloody overthrow of Nuri al-Said and installation of the first independent government in 1958, led by General Abdul al-Qassem, ushered in more political instability. Tensions increased between Arab nationalist and leftist communities in the central government, as well as between Kurdish nationalists reacting to rising Arab *qawmiyya* nationalism. Conflicts between Turcomans, communists, Arabs, and Kurds erupted in Kirkuk in 1959, encouraging sectarian distinctions between the Kurdistan Region and Arab Iraq. Nor were Arab nationalist governments willing aid recipients. Whereas British colonial officers welcomed external assistance, even in a limited form, the revolutionary Arab Ba'athist socialist regime that assumed power in 1968 rejected foreign control of the economy. Iraqi officials accepted international technical assistance as a means of industrializing the state and its petroleum resources, which in turn, strengthened the central government and further isolated the Kurdistan Region.

The emphasis on technical aid to the sovereign Iraqi state, particularly by international lending organizations such as the World Bank, encouraged a particular type of development that helped transition the country from an agrarian-based to an oil-based and semi-industrialized economy. As in the colonial period, the key objectives of state-led development were to improve agricultural productivity and industrialize the country. The central government engaged in land reform, created cooperatives and collective farms, improved conditions for cultivators and farmers, extended irrigation facilities, constructed dams, expanded livestock production, and mechanized the means of production, which included tractor distribution to parts of the Kurdistan Region (Marr 1985, 259). From 1975 to 1985 the amount of land cultivated for tobacco increased from 38,550 to 88,946 *donums*, with production levels rising from 4,457 to 17,222 MT. Agriculture continued to be the main source of economic activity in the Kurdistan Region, with more than half the population dependent upon the agricultural sector and the Kurdish north producing as much as 45 percent of Iraq's wheat needs (Stansfield 2003a, 42).

Yet after 1952 the thrust of externally driven aid was to develop the state's petroleum industry and not to create an agricultural export economy. The central government used international credits and petroleum revenues to construct oil refineries in Khanaqin, Muftryah, and Durra, as well as cement factories in Mosul, Suleymaniya, and Baghdad that produced one million tons of cement annually. Baghdad encouraged investment, industrialization, and petroleum resources, which became the primary source of foreign exchange earnings and the basis of development (Alnasrawi 1991, 14). With the guidance of the Development Board, created in 1950 to direct state-led development, the central government created institutions to finance industry: the Investment Banks of Agriculture, Industry, and Construction. In 1954–55 the Industrial Bank provided 242 loans valued at nearly 1,400,000 Iraqi Swiss dinar (ISD) to private entrepreneurs (Qubain 1958, 184–85; IBRD 1952, 154).[11] By 1956 Iraq had approximately 23,000 industries, the vast majority of which were small establishments engaging five workers or less. Small and medium-sized factories specializing in food and textile items and cigarettes developed for local consumption and regional export (Langley 1961, 90; Hasan 1970, 357; Haj 1997, 61). The first state-supported cigarette factory opened in Suleymaniya city in 1961 and produced 67 percent of total production, or over 430,000 boxes of cigarettes annually (Hussain 2000, 183, 191; Langley 1961, 45).

The transition of the Iraqi economy from semifree enterprise to centralized planning was encouraged by Arab socialism, initiated by the Ba'ath party in 1968. Five-year plans established the framework in which individuals and businesses could operate.[12] These plans nationalized private-sector businesses and placed local industries under state protection so that all budgetary and financial transfers to governorates were made from Baghdad (Alnasrawi 1991, 15). The pace of state-led industrialization increased with the rise in state revenues tied to the nationalization of oil in 1972 and the OPEC crisis the following year. Greater state revenues enabled the Iraqi elite to develop modern transportation

11. Interview with Daro Shaykh Nuri, minister of finance and economics, KRG, Arbil (Hawler), May 15, 1993. The ISD, or OID, was printed in Switzerland and became the officially recognized currency in all of Iraq.

12. Interview with Nowsherwan Mustafa Amin, former secretariat of the PUK and current leader of the Change Movement (Goran), Suleymaniya, Jan. 6, 2006.

and communications that expanded trade and advanced socioeconomic reform, including health care services, education, public-sector employment, and professional opportunities for women (Marr 1985).

Petroleum-based industrialization helped modernize the Iraqi state but wreaked havoc on the agricultural sector, particularly in the Kurdistan Region (Barwari 2002, 68–69). Instead of developing agricultural markets, the government used petroleum revenues to develop a public food distribution system (PDS) based on subsidized food imports (Kirk and Sawdon 2002, 4, 45; Amara 1989, 41–41, 138; Stork 1979, 30, 46; Looney 1992, 616; Marr 1985, 259; Chaudry 2002, 242; Alnasrawi 1991, 12, 74; Mahdi 2002, 16). From 1958 to 1982 development expenditures allocated to agriculture decreased from 38 to 10 percent. The petroleum sector, however, increased from 22 to over 50 percent of the Iraqi national income during the same period (Marr 1985, 249). Over time, the Kurdistan Region lost its role as the country's major food supplier and tax base. By the late 1950s more than two-thirds of Iraq's food needs were imported, with domestic production accounting for about 30 percent. The Kurdish agrarian economy experienced further decline after decades of civil war, the collapse of the Barzani revolution in 1975, the exodus of more than 250,000 Kurds to Iran, the expulsion of villagers to collective towns, and the chemical attacks of the state's Anfal campaign that killed thousands of Kurds and destroyed over four thousand villages (Hiltermann 2007). Chronic instability vacated or destroyed about 80 percent of the rural areas and resulted in a 50 percent decrease in wheat production by 1989 (FAO 2002, 1; Hussain 2000).

State-led industrialization weakened the rural economy but created new opportunities for urban-landowners-turned-businessmen. The mid-1970s represented the golden age of contracting and construction in Iraq, particularly for companies excavating petroleum in southern regions such as Rumaila, Jumhur, Basra, Kirkuk, and Shakir. A symbiotic relationship emerged between the public and private sectors that created a network of linkages between the political elite, private contractors, transportation companies, and local state officials (*mustashars*). Where economic benefits became available, channels of interdependence emerged among businesses in the Kurdistan Region, Baghdad, and Arab-populated regions. Large Kurdish landowners and wealthy businessmen such as Nowruz Khaffaf and Hassib Salah established contracting companies in Baghdad and became urban entrepreneurs, where they lived between economic success and political opposition against the state.[13] Kurdish businessmen also maintained relationships with Iraqi and Arab contracting associations, such as the Arab contractors in Cairo, the Contractors Union of Iraq, and the Iraqi Chamber of Commerce.

Intraregional business linkages continued with the privatization policies of the 1980s, despite the ongoing Iran-Iraq war and Kurdish opposition activities. In the effort to generate revenues and alleviate the state's economic malaise during the war years, the central government permitted the private sector to assume a greater role in economic development. It exempted currency traders from obtaining import licenses, transferred state-owned enterprises to private companies at low prices, reduced taxes, relaxed ownership rights, provided credit extensions to farmers and allowed producers to access wholesale markets (Chaudry 2002, 244; Alnasrawi 1994, 96–99; Leca 1990, 181). These efforts resulted in the sale of more than fifty state-owned manufacturing industries to the private sector (Khudayri 2002, 203; Leca 1990, 181). Privatization had its most important impact on construction activities, which made up as much as 88 percent of the GNP from 1980 to 1987. By 1984 Iraq was exporting cement, sending 2.5 million tons to the Gulf States and 24,000 tons to Jordan (Crusoe 1986, 34–42).

Industrialization and privatization policies in Iraq encouraged urbanization processes and enabled parts of the Kurdistan Region to engage in more complex socioeconomic activities. The development of Mosul as an industrial city offered populations in present-day Dohuk governorate professional opportunities that brought Kurds and Arabs together on a daily basis. Given its geographical proximity, administrative status, and the Arabization policies in the governorate, Dohuk developed important relations with Mosul city and its populations. With only two factories—canning and clothes—created in the 1980s, Kurdish communities from Dohuk moved to Mosul to access employment, skills, and inexpensive

<hr/>

13. Interview with Nowruz Khaffaf, chairman of the Kurdistan Contractors Union, Suleymaniya, Jan. 6, 2006. Khaffaf's grandfather was a wealthy landowner and businessman in Suleymaniya and Baghdad who owned diverse buildings and a chicken farm. In 1974 Khaffaf's company made 1,800,000 OID profit from central government contracts, making him one of the largest and wealthiest Kurdish contractors in Baghdad and the region. While in Baghdad, Khaffaf also provided underground support for PUK *peshmerga* during the war years, which eventually resulted in the confiscation of his personal wealth by Saddam Hussein.

housing. Mosul's four large factories employed about five hundred people each, many of whom were Kurds.[14] Modern transportation routes and administrative linkages facilitated business between Dohuk, Mosul, and the central government. Kurdish businessmen sent their wheat, as well as other food items, to factories in Mosul for production and sales. Nine years after Dohuk became an independent governorate in 1969 it still belonged to the Mosul Chamber of Commerce. Even then, the distinct Dohuk Chamber of Commerce and Industry created in 1978 continued to cooperate with the Mosul branch.

Economic and commercial ties reinforced social and cultural relationships between Kurds and Arabs. In Dohuk and Arbil provinces, most administrative, commercial, and legal issues were conducted in the Arabic language. Kurdish language instruction and schools emerged over time; however, knowledge of Kurdish was minimal and an unnecessary requirement for graduation. Dohuk populations also had access to some of Iraq's best educational institutions in Mosul, including Asharquiya secondary school and Mosul University, established in 1975. Many regularly migrated to Mosul for education, health services, and a better life. Kurdish and Arab families also shared common ties to Islam and participated in Muslim holidays with Sunni Arabs. They traveled to Mosul for Eid al-Fitr to purchase clothes and specialty food items.[15] Similarly, Christian populations in Dohuk and Arbil provinces established cultural, political, and social ties with their counterparts in neighboring Diyala, Mosul, and Baghdad. They depended upon the Arabic language, as well as Syriac, to communicate and had little interaction with or support for the Kurdish nationalist parties.

Business relationships also flourished among certain peasant landowners and private capitalists—those who engaged in mechanized cultivation where private capital and family ownership were dominant, such as Baghdad, Mosul, and parts of Arbil (over 10,000 *donums*)—which benefited from the relative proximity and transportation routes to Mosul. It was in this agriculturally fertile and tribally influential part of the northern region that tractor farming became prominent,

14. Interview with Ayad A. Abdulhalim, chairman, Dohuk Chamber of Commerce, Dohuk, Jan. 3, 2008. Industries in Mosul included the sugar, cement, clothes, and dairy factories.

15. Interviews with Hameed A. Salih, public relations official for the Dohuk governor's office, Dohuk, Jan. 2, 2008, and Ayad A. Abdulhalim, chairman, Dohuk Chamber of Commerce, Dohuk, Jan. 3, 2008, and May 11, 2006.

5. Arbil bazaar, late 1960s–early 1970s. Photograph courtesy of Alwan Antique, Arbil.

land was mechanized, and a new class of merchant landowners, known as the merchant tractorists from Mosul and Arbil, emerged (Haj 1997, 52; IBRD 1952, 141). These types of linkages were less prominent, however, in Suleymaniya province, which had a distinct historical trajectory, more homogenous and literate Kurdish-speaking populations, and different land tenure relations than the more tribalized regions of Dohuk.[16] Merchant and landowning populations in Suleymaniya established commercial, political, and cultural ties with border populations in Kirkuk, Khanquin, and Iranian Kurdistan. Political linkages continued between the urban-educated leftist Kurds, Arab leftists in Baghdad, and the Iraqi Communist Party.

16. From the outset of the state formation period Suleymaniya enjoyed relative autonomy and was permitted to use the Kurdish language for administrative and legal affairs. The Sorani Kurdish dialect of Suleymaniya became the standard and official dialect in the Kurdish educational system, alongside Arabic.

Dependency and Conflict

Despite lucrative business opportunities for privileged entrepreneurs, technical aid to Iraq and petroleum-driven industrialization did not encourage interdependent commercial relations between the Kurdistan Region and Baghdad. The ongoing role of agriculture and continued influence of the Kurdish *agha*, despite land reforms, allowed the tribal tradition to shape patron-client relations in the north, particularly in the Mosul-Ninevah plains. State cooptation policies encouraged tribal leaders to maintain their special relationships with Baghdad through salaries and privileges, further impeding socioeconomic or political reforms and keeping center-periphery linkages confined to individual chieftains and isolated localities (Gerdi 2005, 47; Leezenberg 1999, 10).

Consequently, the Kurdistan Region remained geographically isolated and underdeveloped, just like it was during the early state period. The border town of Zakho, for instance, operated as a small outpost surrounded and controlled by the Iraqi army. Trading activities with Syria, whose political relations with Iraq had become increasingly strained after 1979, were also limited or based on underground economies.[17] In fact, the semiprivate sector that emerged existed only in the shadow of the state. Although private sector activities constituted 72 percent of transportation and communication, companies were generally linked to the regime and the families of Saddam Hussein, who became Iraqi president in 1979 (Leca 1990, 183; Alnasrawi 1994, 97).

State-led development reinforced sectoral and regional distinctions, keeping the Kurdistan Region unrecognized, weak, and dependent. Like other oil-based economies, Iraqi industrial development was capital-intensive and in the form of physical plants and infrastructure such as construction materials, textiles, and food processing (Marr 1985, 243). Whereas the southern and central regions restructured their economies around the industrial and hydrocarbons sectors, and then manufacturing and services, the Kurdistan Region remained tied to an unproductive agricultural sector. Land reforms weakened feudalistic land relationships and created a more equitable land-owning system in some regions;

17. Abdulhalim interview, Jan. 3, 2008.

however, smaller plots brought smaller yields used for individual needs, and not large-scale production. Nor were changes made in land-tenure relations, which impeded efficient land use.

Additionally, as in the early state period, resources and revenues were not proportionately redistributed to the Kurdistan Region from which they were extracted. The central government continued to own most factors of production and sent remittances across provinces. Despite the Kurdistan Region's important oil reserves and natural minerals and suggestions by the IBRD to construct a plant for natural gas and oil in Kirkuk, the central government refused to build a local refinery.[18] Instead, Baghdad sent the petroleum to Dora and Begie in Salahaddin governorate for refining, and then shipped it via pipelines to the Turkish port of Cehan. Marble deposits in Arbil were not treated in the Kurdistan Region, but rather, in a new state-built factory in Haltaniyya, Ramadi. The central government had the marble shipped from Arbil to Mosul and sent to Baghdad.[19] Electricity from the two dams inside the Kurdistan Region was channeled through high-transmission lines to the southern grid and redistributed throughout Iraq.

The wage structure also favored those employed in the petroleum industry in cities in central and southern regions, and not the rural Kurdistan areas. Skilled laborers were concentrated in Baghdad, where the average income was one-fourth higher than in the north. Government-led industrial development boomed after 1964; however, 52 percent of small industry and 78 percent of large industry remained centered in key cities such as Baghdad, Basra, and Mosul (Marr 1985, 270; Khudayri 2002, 202). Although the Kurdistan Region had the two largest cement factories and 142 small factories with 13,929 workers, they represented less than 8 percent of the total number of factories and workers

18. Oil was first produced in Kirkuk in 1927 in Baba Gurgur and Ain Zala. The Iraqi central government exported oil through the main, northern pipeline system (Banias and Tripoli in Syria and Lebanon) on the Mediterranean coast, to Turkey through the Iraqi-Turkish line to the Terminal Porto, Cehan, and the Mediterranean and to Basra southward through the strategic line at Haditha. From this southern port the petroleum was exported through two sea terminals: the deep terminal of al-Bakir and the terminal of Khor al-Amaya (MERA 2007).

19. Interview with Awat Barzinji, former manager of Galala Trading Company and marketing and projects director, The Kar Group, Arbil, Jan. 13, 2007.

in Iraq (Barwari 2002).[20] Most industries in the Kurdistan Region were family owned and based on personal services such as grain milling, baking, metal and shoe repair, textiles, carpentry, and jewelry (Langley 1961, 281). Social services were equally underdeveloped and disproportionately allocated. Although the Kurdistan Region had thirty-two hospitals (of 252), or about 33 percent of the total in Iraq, these facilities lacked equipment, competent staff, and medicines. Kindergarten and primary schools in the Kurdistan Region represented about 12 percent of the country's total, whereas high schools represented about 5 percent, with only one university established in 1968 (Barwari 2002).[21]

Absence of industrialization and urbanization processes prevented the diversification of social groupings outside the family, tribe, or ethnicity (Marr 1985, 271). Whereas the central regions of Iraq became more complex, with an urban upper class composed of entrepreneurs and businessmen tied to the land, a middle class defined by its secular education and its mixture of professionals, and lower classes employed in large-scale factories and modern industries, the Kurdistan Region remained a traditional society characterized by immediate survival strategies in a state-run economy, religion, and a sense of communality (Inglehart 1997, 76; Marr 1985, 137). The influence of traditional sociopolitical structures hindered attitudinal changes that could have advanced rationalization and bureaucratization.

To be sure, state-engineered development differentials coincided with the rise of urban centers in the Kurdistan Region, whose populations increased by 35 percent from 1965 to 1987 (Ahmed 1993, 3). Demographic changes occurred alongside Arabization policies and decades of civil war, which transformed borders and administrative units and reshaped territories, populations, and intercommunal relations. Yet, unlike urbanization processes that occurred in central Iraq or Mosul, which had given rise to more literate and diversified workforces, in the Kurdistan Region they resulted in greater unemployment and isolation. The Iraqi state petrolized the economy as the Kurds were expelled from their homes,

---

20. Interviews with Arar A. Karim, chairman of the Suleymaniya Department of Industry, Mar. 1, 2006, Suleymaniya and Rashad Ahmad Ibrahim, department manager and trader, Chamber of Commerce and Industry, Ministry of Economics and Finance, KRG, Arbil, Jan. 1994.

21. The University of Suleymaniya was established in 1968 and transferred to Arbil in 1982. Its name was then changed to the University of Salahaddin.

as villages were bombed, as borders were redrawn, and as the central government repressed opponents of the state. Kirkuk became the target of forced expulsions and state military repression. In contrast to the colonial period, whereby the distribution of power was based on population percentages, after the late 1960s it became focused on Arab ethnicity. Saddam Hussein forced all non-Arab groups in Kirkuk to sign ethnic identity correction cards, register officially as Arabs, and join the Ba'ath army. They were hired by the government and worked against Kurds, and they therefore were considered *jash* (traitors) by Kurds. Kurds and Turcomans were fired from administrative posts and replaced with Arabs, who gained positions and housing privileges at the Northern Petroleum Company (NPC) in the city center. The ongoing sense of instability and political climate of fear instilled by Saddam Hussein and the Ba'athists created a sense of vulnerability and uncertainty that prevented long-term investment or development in the region (FAO 2002, 8).

These processes impacted households by causing the forced displacement of Kurds to collective towns, refugee camps, and abroad, which weakened the traditional way of life, changed consumption patterns, and increased state dependency. By 1990, about 700,000 Faili Kurds had taken refuge in Baghdad, 250,000 Barzani Kurds had fled to Iran, and 200,000 others had joined other diasporic communities, mainly in Europe. An additional 300,000 Kurds had been displaced from Kirkuk to central and southern Iraq and city centers in Arbil and Suleymaniya, where they became part of a growing internally displaced populations (Atlasi Kirkuk 2006, 64).[22] Population displacements and transformations in the political economy shaped prospects for development by setting the expectations of local populations as to what the state should provide (Wiarda 2004; Fukayama 2002, 26; Krishna 2002, 58–59). Forced expulsions and migrations of rural populations to towns and cities not only broke a key sector of the local economy and strengthened the growing sense of Kurdish nationalism, but also

22. In 1957–77 the percentage of Kurds in Kirkuk decreased from 48 to 37 percent, while Arab populations increased from 28 to 44 percent. About 20 percent of the total population in Kirkuk comprised Arab tribes, 70 percent of which originated from central and southern Iraq. The Turcoman-populated Duz Khormatu and Kifri districts were transferred to Tikrit (Salahaddin) and Diyala respectively. Kurdish-populated Kalar and Chamchamal districts were transferred to Suleymaniya.

created pathologies of victimization and dependency within Kurdish society. Without access to land and employment and with no obligation to pay taxes, the Kurds went from being self-sufficient agricultural producers to sycophants of the Iraqi social welfare state. People stopped working because their land was destroyed, they refused to be members of the Ba'ath party, or there were no avenues for a private sector. Students stopped learning because the Ba'athist system was based on *wasta*—personal contacts—and not individual merit-based skills.

Given the demands of the Kurdistan Region and the availability of an international aid regime, one would have expected foreign intervention and assistance to Iraqi Kurds as victims of state repression and conflict. The 1973 U.S. Foreign Assistance Act represented a key shift in U.S. aid policy from technical assistance to meeting the basic human needs of the poor (Ruttan 1996, 95, 444). One of the main objectives of the expanded USAID mission was to provide technical and financial assistance to developing countries as a means of improving their institutional capabilities (Rondinelli 1987, 2). By the 1980s INGOs, development agencies,

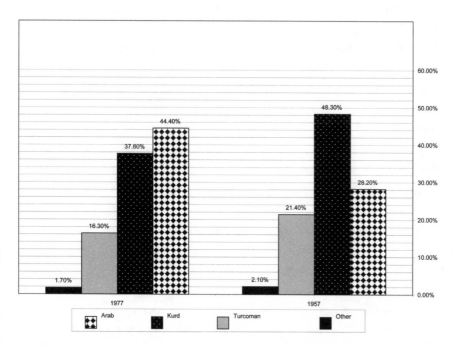

6. Ethnic composition of the population of Kirkuk governorate, 1957–77. *Source:* MERA 2007.

universities, and human-rights organizations had proliferated around the globe, focusing on war-torn countries such as Africa, Afghanistan, and Central America.

Yet no foreign government or international organization attempted to use aid as a means of mitigating conflict, stabilizing the Iraqi regime, reducing poverty, or creating viable institutions in the Kurdistan Region. Even during the numerous ceasefires in the 1960s or the 1970 March Manifesto, the agreement between Baghdad and the Kurdistan Region to negotiate political autonomy for the Kurds, there were no peacekeeping missions, conflict-resolution strategies, or conferences in foreign capitals to encourage confidence-building measures between the Kurds and the central government. Nor was any large-scale effort made to advocate human rights, protect the Kurds from Saddam Hussein's genocidal Anfal campaign, or negotiate Kirkuk. Although the Reagan administration was clearly aware that the Iraqi government had used chemical agents against the Kurds and had eradicated villages and rural areas in the Kurdish border areas during the Iran-Iraq war, it considered Baghdad's repression of the Kurds as an internal affair (Hiltermann 2007, 100–103). Until the late 1980s U.S. interests in the Middle East focused on resolving the Arab-Israel problem and not the Kurdish issue in Iraq (Ruttan 1996, 300).

To be sure, during the civil war period of the 1960s Kurdish factions received financial support from the governments of the United States, Israel, and Iran against rising Arab nationalism. This assistance offered some form of unofficial external recognition, increased Kurdish wartime capabilities, and semi-legitimized the Kurdish leadership and political parties, who administered their opposition-cum-autonomy movement from their mountain headquarters. The Russian government also intervened in the attempt to quell potential violence, while institutions such as the Organization for Arab States (OAS) sponsored conferences in the region.

Still, international assistance to the Kurds was clandestine and temporary. It was driven by the strategic interests of foreign governments that continued to focus on petroleum revenues in the sovereign Iraqi state, no matter how illegitimate it had become, and not the unrecognized Kurdistan Region. International actors and their oil industries also regarded Iraq as a moderate, secular, Middle Eastern regime that could be tolerated for economic and security reasons (Ruttan 1996, 300). During and immediately after the Iran-Iraq war, the U.S. government's pro-Iraq tilt and policy of "constructive engagement" supported its overriding interests in securing a significant role for American business in "a substantial post-war reconstruction effort" (Hiltermann 2007, 217). Thus, instead of sanctioning the Iraqi regime for human rights violations and use of chemical weapons against Kurdish populations, the U.S. government restored diplomatic relations with Iraq and commenced a lucrative weapons trade with its Western defense contractors and the Iraqi central government. A U.S. delegation met with Saddam Hussein in Mosul on April 2, 1990, emphasizing its government's interest in improving relations with Iraq (Natali 2001, 276).

Regional states also remained committed to state sovereignty, which required quelling nationalist and separatist movements and not assisting vulnerable populations in the Kurdistan Region. To ensure profits from petroleum agreements with the Iraqi government and to control its civil war with the PKK, the Turkish government signed a hot-pursuit agreement with Baghdad in April 1983 authorizing search and seizure of terrorists in the northern border areas. Syria and Iran had their own Kurdish nationalist populations to control as well and refused long-term sustainable assistance to the Iraqi Kurds.

Certainly, even if humanitarian assistance was directly available, the authoritarian, centralized Iraqi state and unstable Kurdish north would have had no institutional capabilities to sustain effective aid distribution or long-term development. The country still had no legitimate constitution that respected the political rights of the Kurds or minority groups. The autonomy agreement declared by Saddam Hussein and rejected by Mullah Mustafa Barzani in 1974 provided for a Baghdad-appointed administration in which Kurdish representatives had no participation in decision making or policy implementation. Although the Law of Self-Rule (no. 33) provided limited institutions of governance, channels of participation remained closed at the local levels. The Ba'athist regime and its security apparatus controlled trade unions, civil-society organizations, and youth groups, preventing the devolution of power to the provinces or the expression of individual liberties. Provincial governors had no authority in politics or the courts and were seconded to the security office in Baghdad.[23] Numerous leftist and Kurdish nationalist parties eventually emerged in the late 1970s, including

23. Interview with Mr. Ahmad, Directorate of Planning, Ministry of Finance, KRG, Arbil, Nov. 27, 2007.

Jelal Talabani's PUK. These groups, however, lacked resources or mechanisms of support to maintain local governance. They also operated clandestinely as an isolated Kurdistan Front (KF), either in people's homes or from caves in the mountainous border regions. The *peshmerga* mountain management mentality that emerged from this historical context, as well as illiterate populations tied to traditional social structures, further prevented institution building and any form of internal sovereignty for the Kurdistan Region.

Moreover, by the late 1980s, political trust between the Kurdistan Region and Baghdad was virtually nonexistent. Most Kurdish villages and key towns had been demolished and their populations transferred to collective towns. The region remained isolated and without viable political institutions or a stake in the global, regional, or national economies. People were seeking international recognition as victims of Saddam Hussein and not ways to become part of the Iraqi state. The only interest and leverage the Kurds had in Iraq was sabotaging pipelines, engaging in military reprisals, and allying with radical cross-border nationalist groups and foreign governments to advance their short-term interests.

Conclusions

The nature of foreign aid in the prewar period focused on technical assistance to the Iraqi state and not the underdeveloped and unrecognized Kurdistan Region, which allowed differentiated development processes to continue over time. Whereas the Iraqi economy benefited from the dynamic changes that pushed development from the late nineteenth to mid–twentieth century, allowing it to acquire foreign capital and penetrate world markets with petroleum resources, the Kurdistan Region remained disconnected from the world economy and politics. International and regional isolation discouraged positive, sustainable relations from developing between the Kurdistan Region and Baghdad. Those areas in which commercial, cultural, and social ties developed were limited to pockets of regions where industry had emerged and where Kurds had opportunities to integrate into the local economy, such as Mosul and Baghdad. Political liaisons were mainly among small communities of businessmen, privileged families, political elite, and tribal leaders acting as middlemen, *jash,* or Ba'athist representatives in the region, and not between the larger Kurdistan Region and its populations.

2

The Relief Phase

THE 1990 PERSIAN GULF WAR and its subsequent aid programs rescaled the development trajectory of the Kurdistan Region. Foreign assistance targeted not only the sovereign Iraqi state but also the Kurds as victims of Saddam Hussein. International aid created a relatively stable environment that permitted economic recovery, rehabilitation, and institution building. It also offered the Kurdistan Region forms of recognition, external patronage, and internal sovereignty that encouraged quasi-statehood. During this period the Kurds conducted elections, created their own government, and engaged in civil society building. They also re-created map images of "Free Kurdistan." These efforts at strengthening Kurdish autonomy, however, were checked by the nature of the aid program, which assured the territorial integrity of Iraq and not a self-sustaining Kurdistan Region. Political culture and domestic structural constraints also continued to frustrate long-term development, and in many instances, impeded external assistance programs. Highly dependent upon international aid, still isolated from world markets, and lacking mechanisms of integration, the only linkages that could be sustained with Baghdad were based on ongoing political distrust, illicit trade, and limited sociocultural exchanges.

Protecting the Kurds

In contrast to the prewar period, whereby the Kurdistan Region had no access to foreign assistance, the international aid regime that commenced after the Persian Gulf War offered Iraqi Kurds new forms of patronage and support. It reflected changes in international politics and the strategic interests of the first Bush administration (1989–93), the UN, and foreign governments, which centered on protecting world petroleum markets, preventing the spread of WMD in

Iraq, and controlling the reckless political behavior of Saddam Hussein (Tripp 2007, 249–50). Humanitarian relief to the Kurds also was linked to larger transformations in the aid regime that challenged the notion of state sovereignty and focused on protecting local populations on human rights principles and demands for postconflict recovery.

In particular, external aid to the Kurdistan Region was a direct response to the failed Kurdish uprising against Saddam Hussein in April 1991. The mass exodus of about two million Kurds to the mountainous regions of Turkey and Iran created a humanitarian crisis that stirred international pressure for foreign intervention. UN sanctions imposed against Iraq, Baghdad's internal embargo against the Kurdistan Region, and Saddam Hussein's authoritarian rule exacerbated the situation and caused increased hardship to local populations (Baram 2000, 20; Alnasrawi 2001, 205–18). With the approval of UNSCR 688, the three governorates in the Kurdistan Region gained international security protection in the form of a safe haven and no-fly zone, implemented by coalition forces as part of Operation Provide Comfort II (OPC) (Graham-Brown 1999, 105–11; McQueen 2005, 24–28). The coalition maintained a small military presence at the Military Coordination Center (MCC) in the border town of Zakho, serving as a liaison center for INGOs and the U.S. Office of Foreign Disaster Assistance (OFDA), a branch of the USAID and leading donor agency the Kurdistan Region.

Humanitarian aid also commenced en masse, replacing state welfare assistance and becoming the most important source of the region's external finance. Given the impediments toward effective aid delivery in Saddam-controlled regions of central and southern Iraq, the needs of Kurdish refugees, and the relatively safe climate in the Kurdistan Region, aid revenues were skewed toward the Kurdish north. From 1991 to 1996 the Kurdistan Region received approximately two-thirds of total aid assistance, or over US$1 billion in goods and services (Natali 2007c, 1112–13; Carapico 2002; Graham-Brown 2002, 272; Stansfield 2003a, 52; USAID 2003). Other funds were provided as bilateral and multilateral assistance, the majority of which was allocated at the outbreak of the Gulf War in 1991, earmarked for particular UN agencies or channeled through the OFDA. The British Overseas Development Administration, which became the Department for International Development, allocated 78 percent of its Iraq program budget to the northern region, and only 22 percent to southern and central Iraq. The UN, whose operations were based in Baghdad, spent 65 percent of its total

Iraqi funding in the Kurdistan Region (Graham-Brown 2002, 277). By 1994–95, after having refused to sign the Memorandum of Understanding (MOU) with the Iraqi government, about fifty INGOs were working in the Kurdistan Region, while only four were established in southern and central Iraq (Graham-Brown 2002, 271–73).

International assistance to willing aid recipients encouraged relative stability, economic recovery, and rehabilitation. Despite the difficult postwar living conditions, including power outages, food shortages, and unemployment, local populations were euphoric about their new political freedoms. Their open attitude toward foreign aid, direct presence of donor agencies and coalition forces in Zakho, and the U.S.-funded program that supported small projects created a receptive environment for aid distribution.[1] INGOs constructed schools and hospitals in rural areas, procured educational materials and medicines, paid teachers' salaries, implemented school feeding programs, rebuilt access roads, and resettled nearly two million Kurdish refugees to their original villages or urban housing. UN water and sanitation projects (WATSAN) affected about 90 percent of the total villages in the Kurdistan Region.[2] Over time, new development differentials started to emerge. While the Saddam-controlled, aid-restricted regions experienced spiraling inflation, political instability, and socioeconomic decline, the Kurdistan Region had resettled most refugees, rehabilitated some rural areas, and assured some basic needs for local populations.

Different sectors of the economy slowly revived. Whereas agricultural production had weakened in the prewar period, particularly during the Iran-Iraq war, after 1992 it gradually improved. Production was stimulated by the U.S. government–funded wheat buy-back program,[3] implemented by the OFDA and

1. Although the main role of the MCC was to provide security to the region, it coordinated with the OFDA Disaster Assistance Relief Team (DART) and engaged in procurement and project assessment activities. OFDA Zakho offices were also located in the MCC compound, which encouraged close working relationships between the two organizations, as well as with INGOs, which received payments for small projects directly from the MCC paymaster on a regular basis.

2. Interview with Khawla Ra'ouf Khanekah, assistant project officer, UNICEF, Arbil, May 24, 2006.

3. OFDA initiated the U.S.-funded wheat procurement plan in the Kurdistan Region on July 25, 1993, to purchase the maximum amount of the wheat harvest from local farmers, preposition

the World Food Programme (WFP) as a means of assisting local farmers by purchasing locally produced wheat at competitive market prices. From 1990 to 1995 the purchase price of wheat increased by 50 percent, from US$60 to US$290 per MT, while the area cultivated with grains increased by 52 percent, with production doubling from about 340,000 to 665,000 MT annually (FAO 2003, 1, 98; Kirk and Sawdon 2002, 9–11; Barwari 2002; Stansfield 2003a, 56; Gazdar and Hussain 2002, 47).[4]

Postwar recovery and the external patronage it accorded to the Kurds had unintended consequences on institution building (Carapico 2002; Graham-Brown 2002; DiPrizio 2002, 30; Brown 2003, 142). Influenced by the benefits of U.S.-sponsored democratization movements in Eastern Europe and attempting to fill the power vacuum in the north, the KF descended from its mountain strongholds to manage political affairs in the cities. Despite internal disagreements over the type of electoral processes to be applied in the region, in May 1992 Kurdish officials conducted elections and created the first KRG, based in Arbil.[5] In contrast to the Baghdad-appointed administration established in the

cereal supplies, and sustain food distributions during the winter period. Under the program, the WFP aimed to procure 40,000–50,000 MT of grade-two wheat at US$140 per MT in various stages. An initial US$2 million was made available with another $8 million available pending successful activities.

4. The pre–Gulf War government procurement price for class-one wheat was 270 ID (about US$60) per MT, and fluctuated between US$50 and US$90 from 1994 to 1995, and then increased with the appreciation of the U.S. dollar in 1996, to US$100. The set local price for wheat was US$120, established by local market companies and based on demand. Of this amount $37 went to a middleman, $27 to the KRG, and $10 for a silo tax. The remaining $46 was used to purchase the wheat. Production was also influenced by regional pricing. For example, when the harvest was good in Turkey and price was set at US$170–80 per MT, with an additional US$20 for transportation costs, merchants in neighboring Dohuk province had less interest in selling to Turkey. In Suleymaniya, proper cleaning materials were unavailable and the Iranian *toman* was strong, so wheat was purchased across borders.

5. The election selected a leader and national assembly for the Kurdistan Region. Ma'soud Barzani received 25,863 more votes than Jelal Talabani, although neither candidate secured the majority necessary to control the leadership position. After reallocating votes of five parties that did not achieve the 7 percent threshold, the KDP obtained only 1.6 percent more votes than the PUK. It then ceded one of its assembly votes to the PUK, giving each party fifty seats in the KNA. Article 1 of the electoral law (formation of the assembly) stated that "the Iraqi Kurdistan National

1970s, the Kurdish regional government in Arbil was a Kurdish-run operation that attempted to provide the institutional framework for self-rule. Grounded in the "50–50 split," it was based on a governance system that shared and separated power between the KDP and PUK, while allowing small representation for one Christian party (Hoff, Leezenberg, and Muller 1992; "Ballots Without Borders" 1992; ELKLM 1992; ELKNA 1992; THCSEK 1992).[6] Thus, a KDP minister was obliged to have a PUK deputy minister while a PUK minister had to have a KDP deputy. This arrangement capitalized on the nationalist fervor of the time; however, its real objective was to fill the power vacuum, maintain unity between the two fractious parties, and stabilize the region.

Kurdish quasi-state building was further influenced by democratic norms imported from abroad. Immediately after the war, a group of diasporic Kurdish lawyers prepared a constitution and what it perceived were institutional guidelines in which a modern parliamentary political system could be sustained—a speaker of the house, president of the Kurdistan National Assembly (KNA), and expanded ministerial cabinet to include four newly created ministries: reconstruction and development, humanitarian aid and cooperation, *peshmerga* affairs, and culture (Talabani 1993).[7] During the first premiership of Fuad Massoum, the KRG devised government programs, fortified its *peshmerga*, and established a council of governors at the provincial level to liaise with INGOs,

---

Assembly shall consist of no less than 100 members on the basis of one representative for each 30,000 people."

6. The power-sharing system, called the "50–50 split," was based on an agreement by Ma'soud Barzani and Jelal Talabani and their political parties to share the leadership position and seats in the first KRG, with five seats allocated to the Assyrian Democratic Movement (ADM). Nearly all aspects of political affairs, including hospitals, police departments and checkpoints, were split "50–50."

7. Interview with Nuri Talabani, independent member of the Kurdistan parliament, Arbil, Apr. 5, 2007. In 1992 the first draft of the constitution was prepared by thirty-three members of the parliament from the KDP and PUK, as well as Nuri Talabani. In referring to the president of the region, the members initially wanted to use the term "Raber"—which is used in Iran to designate the leader elected directly by the people. However, Nuri Talabani sent an open letter to the Kurdistan Front arguing not to accept it so as to prevent the Kurdistan Region becoming a theocracy like Iran. The term "Raberî Bazutneweyeh Kurdayetî"—leader of the Kurdish movement—was then replaced with president of the Kurdistan Region.

the UN, and donor agencies (Natali 1999).[8] It also created the legal framework in which to integrate civil society into local authority structures, including laws that expanded the rights of ethnic and religious minorities and procedures for public demonstrations. Trade unions, youth groups, media agencies, and local NGOs emerged and started to mobilize for educational reform, women's rights, and individual freedoms. In Suleymaniya, some demonstrators protested against political party rivalries, which led to a series of public debates and promises from the KRG to protect "democratization in Kurdistan."[9]

Kurdish officials also started using a new political discourse, describing their emergent quasi-state as "Free Kurdistan" (Natali 2001, 282). To this end, the KRG engaged in identity-reshaping projects that Kurdified or de-Arabized the education, administrative, and communication systems. Curricula, street signs, and communiqués were changed from Arabic to the Kurdish language. Television stations, newspapers, and universities were created or reopened, all based on the Kurdish language and history and underlined by nationalist themes. The tacit approval of these processes by foreign governments and international organizations, alongside continued authoritarian rule and ostracization of Saddam Hussein, semi-legitimized the Kurdish quasi-state and reinforced its sense of virtual separation from Baghdad.

Maintaining the Status Quo

A generous aid regime supported economic recovery and institution building in the Kurdistan Region. Yet the highly politicized nature of aid and its funding mechanisms placed conditionalities on the type of projects that could be implemented, which checked the internal sovereignty of the Kurdish quasi-state,

---

8. Interview with Kemal Mufti, minister of *peshmerga* affairs, Arbil, Feb. 18, 1993. By March 1993 the KRG had a security force of over 30,000 *peshmerga*, 7,000 police forces, and a reserve of 5,000 forces that remained in party control.

9. Official response by the president of the Kurdistan National Assembly, Jawer Namik on Kurdistan TV, Dec. 16, 1993. The demonstrations were organized in Suleymaniya in December 1993 by a local human rights organization, in coordination with PUK supporters. They were in protest against the armed clashes between the KDP and the Kurdistan Socialist Party (KSP), headed by Mohammed Haji Mahmoud.

reinforced the status quo, and prevented long-term development. From the outset of the aid program, UN member-states were concerned about violating article 2 (7) of the UN Charter that committed the world body to the territorial integrity of Iraq. Even though UNSCR 688 set the legal framework for protecting the Kurdistan Region against future encroachments by Saddam Hussein, the issue of Iraqi sovereignty, even in its weakened form, remained a sensitive one. The UN sanctions committee in New York also kept tight control of the goods entering or leaving Iraq, prohibiting petroleum exports and limiting imports to selected foodstuffs and relief supplies.

Given the commitment to Iraqi sovereignty and conditionalities of the sanctions regime the UN, foreign governments, and donor agencies pursued a one-Iraq policy that treated the Kurdistan Region like the rest of the country. They did not officially recognize the KRG as a legitimate government, despite its increasingly evident de facto status and the defunct government in Baghdad. INGOs also were prohibited from channeling funds to the KRG or public institutions in the Kurdistan Region, which prevented training and integrating public-sector professionals into rehabilitation processes. Indeed, some INGOs worked closely with the KRG Ministry of Reconstruction and Development (MORAD) as part of rural rehabilitation and resettlement programs. Others coordinated with local NGOs that were linked to high-ranking officials or the political parties.

Still, the KRG was locked out of key public sector projects, which limited any internal sovereignty leverage it could have had within the Iraqi state and inside the Kurdistan Region. The UN humanitarian program in Iraq was equally exclusionary. Six-month program and funding reviews made by UN headquarters in New York prevented long-term planning or development projects. By requiring final approval of staff and projects in the Kurdistan Region by the central government, the UN marginalized the KRG from programming while allowing the Ba'athist regime indirect control of the Kurdish north.

Aid conditionalities also were shaped by the government of Turkey and its strategic relationship with western governments, particularly the United States (Graham-Brown 1999, 222, 310). Turkey controlled the only open border-crossing point into Iraqi Kurdistan (Khabur; Ibrahim Khalil on the Kurdish side) through which humanitarian aid could pass. It had final decision-making power on the use of its military base in Incirlik, which served as a staging point for U.S. aircraft operating the no-fly zone over parts of the Kurdistan Region. This arrangement, renewable every six months, kept the security and U.S. humanitarian aid program functioning on biannual contingency plans dependent upon approval by Ankara (Natali 1999). Additionally, the Turkish government had its own Kurdish problem to manage, particularly during the ongoing civil war with the PKK, and was highly sensitive to the idea of an autonomous Kurdistan Region. As part of its ongoing agreement with the Iraqi central government to "search and seize terrorists" in border areas, the Turkish military engaged in military incursions in the Kurdistan Region. It bombed Kurdish border areas and villages suspected of harboring the PKK, pressured Western governments against supporting or recognizing Iraqi Kurdistan, and obstructed relief operations. Turkish officials sporadically closed the border and prevented humanitarian goods and personnel from entering or leaving the Kurdistan Region, which often led to shortages, strikes, and price increases.

As a result, U.S. strategic interests, regional pressures, and political expediency became the guidelines for addressing the aid program in the Kurdish north. The creation of the safe haven was more a by-product of external influences, media coverage, and the need to resettle Kurdish refugees than it was a planned effort to protect and develop the Kurdistan Region over the long term. One of the main concerns of the U.S. government in the aftermath of the Gulf War was to assure Turkey that Kurdish refugees would be resettled from the Turkish-Iraqi border and kept inside Iraq. The underlying policy of OPC was that U.S. intervention was a short-term measure and that U.S. programs would eventually be transitioned to the United Nations (Chorev 2007, 53; DiPrizio, 2002 26–33, Graham-Brown 1999, 105–21, 144).

Instead of initiating the self-sustainability measures advocated in most post-conflict settings, the program constrained them in the Kurdistan Region (Milas and Latif, 2000, 371).[10] No effort was made to promote local capacity building, despite weak institutions and the absence of social capital. Most U.S. funds came from the Department of Defense (DOD), which had its own rules for disbursement based on material goods and logistics that created a "commodity-driven" approach focused on food and fuel distributions (Graham-Brown 1999, 278–84).

---

10. Postconflict rehabilitation in Ethiopia during this same period encouraged economic revival with macroeconomic reform, which included exchange-rate stabilization, increasing private investment, and developing industrial and service sectors.

Even UNICEF, the UN agency specialized in children and health services, distributed kerosene and potable water as part of its humanitarian assistance program in the north.

Aid conditionalities limited the region's development potential. For example, although the wheat buy-back program assisted local farmers and encouraged agricultural production, it did not permit KRG participation, which hindered the potential transfer of skills to local officials. Rather than coordinating wheat procurements directly with Kurdish authorities, donor agencies gave CARE Australia the authority to store, measure, and distribute the wheat. Small local contractors were locked out of the bidding process because one of the conditionalities of the program was that a potential contractor had to have a bank account in Turkey. Donors also set local purchase prices according to the international market price for wheat without fully understanding local politics, regional economies, and the impact of the program on Kurdish farmers. The functioning of a two-tier exchange rate in Iraq, lack of sufficient storage facilities, and exportation of wheat to neighboring states that paid higher prices reduced the availability of local crops. Despite the increase of cultivated agricultural lands during this period and benefits to agricultural producers, many local farmers hoarded their crops for personal use or exported them to Iran or Turkey.

Indeed, the conditions and needs of postwar Iraqi Kurdistan warranted short-term disaster relief and not development aid. Hundreds of thousands of refugees had to be resettled; potable water, food and fuel had to be distributed; bridges had to be built; and basic services had to be established to ensure the immediate survival of local populations. The central government's canceling of its social welfare services and replacement with a system of subsidized rations not only terminated public sector salaries, but also led to price increases and currency fluctuations. Local populations that benefited from the strong prewar ISD saw their earnings decline significantly during this period (Gazdar and Hussain 2002, 40, 55). After Saddam Hussein removed the twenty-five-ISD note from circulation in May 1993 and created a "photocopied" (*muzarrat*) currency for regions south of the green line, many people lost their life savings and ceased using local banks altogether. Different exchange rates and local economies that emerged may have benefited the Kurdistan Region; however, the economic precariousness weakened confidence in public-sector institutions, particularly the banking system. It also limited the options for the KRG to engage in local development initiatives (Natali 1999; Gazdar and Hussain 2002, 40).

Political conditions undermined potential development, just as they did in the prewar period. Despite international security protection, the no-fly zone and safe haven only included parts of the Kurdistan Region and offered no real assurance against internal conflict or regional security threats. Unexpected crises, such as border closings by the Turkish government, mass migrations of over 14,000 Kurdish refugees from Turkey into the Kurdistan Region, PKK reprisals, and attacks by Baghdad against INGO workers created security constraints that hindered or terminated humanitarian aid project activities. UN

TABLE 1. MARKET PRICES OF MAJOR COMMODITIES
IN THE KURDISTAN REGION, APRIL 1993–JULY 1994 (ISD).

Item	April 1993	Dec. 1993	July 1994	% change
Wheat (MT)[a]	4,250	7,710	8,600	+102
Flour (50kg)[a]	285	560	650	+128
Sugar (50kg)[a]	450	980	1,540	+242
Rice (50kg)	430	830	1,300	+202
Chickpeas (1kg)	6	10	30	+400
Vegetable oil (1kg)[a]	19	41	57	+200
Benzine (L)	3	3	7	+133
Diesel (L)	2	3	1	-50
Exchange rate ISD				
US$1	25	52	72	-188
Turkish lira 50,000	122	172	113	+7
Iranian toman	n/a	4	3.2	+200
"Fake" ID:USD	n/a	138	489	-589
Gold (1g)	250	565	755	202

Source: Natali, Denise. 1999. "International Aid, Regional Politics and the Kurdish Issue in Iraq Since the Persian Gulf War," The Emirates Occasional Papers, No. 31, Abu Dhabi: The Emirates Center for Strategic Studies and Research, 21.

Notes: Prices are calculated for the three governorates in the Kurdistan Region. The Turkish lira is used for commercial trade in Dohuk governorate, and the Iranian toman is used in Suleymaniya and at times in Arbil (Hawler) for trading purposes.

[a]Wheat, flour, sugar, and vegetable oil are imported from Turkey. Prices are about 10 percent lower in Dohuk than in Suleymaniya owing to transportation costs and internal customs taxes.

trucks from Baghdad traveling through Mosul governorate were sporadically bombed or looted, which often delayed the distribution of goods and services inside the Kurdistan Region. Pressures from Syria and Iranian military attacks against Iranian Kurdish dissidents often resulted in cross-border and internal conflicts with Iraqi Kurdish parties, the Iranian Pasdaran, and the Islamic Movement of Kurdistan (IMK), which was influential in the Girmian region of Suleymaniya and the border area of Halabja.[11] Interparty pressures, added to ongoing disagreements between the KDP and PUK over the allocation of resources, unsettled local politics and prevented some projects from being realized.[12] Certain conflict-prone regions often became too unstable and ineligible for continuous aid allocations.

Nor did the emergent Kurdish quasi-state have the appropriate mechanisms and institutional foundations from which aid could have been effectively distributed (Rondinelli 1987, 3). Despite important water and petroleum resources, the Kurdish north suffered from decades of war, Anfal operations, and neglect of the infrastructure. The Persian Gulf War destroyed the backbone of the telecommunications system, including national microwave, cable, and rural telephone networks. Resource linkages were further disrupted when the Kurds dismantled the electrical lines from the Darbandikan and Dokan dams and Saddam cut electricity to Dohuk governorate, which reduced the capacities of the dams and substations and impeded water and electricity flows between the regions. Even though Kurdish engineers established a relatively autonomous power system for parts of the region in 1995, it worked at minimal capacity. The region also lacked a credible education system, health care services, and skilled

11. Interview with Mohammed Towfiq, minister of humanitarian affairs, Suleymaniya, June 17, 1994. Iran also supported the Hezbollah movement in Choman and Dohuk and the IMK in Halabja. The leader of the Hezbollah movement in Iraqi Kurdistan was Adham Barzani, the cousin of Ma'soud Barzani. The Hezbollah movement is a small group involved in trading activities in the Choman Valley, along the Iraqi-Kurdish-Iranian border. It is distinct from the Kurdish Hezbollah movement in southeast Turkey.

12. For instance, after the thirteenth KDP congress, the KSP left the KDP alliance and joined the PUK. Although the KSP was a small party, its leader, Hama Haji Mahmoud, was supported by Iran. Similarly the IMK, led by Mullah Othman, allied with the KDP, which gave KDP influence in Halabja, a religiously mixed town in the Hawraman-Iranian border area neighboring Suleymaniya province.

bureaucracy, leaving it at nearly the same level of underdevelopment it was at in the prewar period and without the capabilities to implement sustainable development projects.

Domestic structural constraints further challenged development and reform. Traditional power structures kept the sociopolitical system highly stratified and the division of labor nonspecialized. Individuals remained relatively isolated from the outside world, preventing more complex social relationships from emerging outside the family unit (Ingelhart 1997, 90; Smelser 1971, 354). Endogamous family relations, lack of positive social capital associated with market economies, and party monopolization of politics and society limited the extent to which an independent civil society could develop, despite the local NGOs that had become active at this time. Absence of forces of integration and the persistence of a bazaar-cash economy also prevented the creation of a "modern personality" or the attitudinal changes needed to support the transition from traditional ways of thinking to more rational and scientific ones (Inglehart 1997, 54; Dube 1988, 2, 18–24).[13] For instance, as in the prewar period, risk-averse landowners still preferred to hoard money in their homes instead of supporting local investment projects. Uneducated farmers often refused pesticides until it was too late to prevent crop disease, such as sunna pest. One of the consequences was stunted rural development. Agriculture remained based on subsistence farming and not the commercial production of goods or specialization of cash crops (Smelser 1971, 352).

Nor were the Kurdish elites interested in altering traditional power structures as a means of reforming society and politics. Although the KRG was modeled after a parliamentary system, it was essentially a refabricated version of the KF and mired in party rivalries. The parliament had no opposition party, no prime minister able to dismiss the government, and no real authority outside the antiquated Soviet-style political party politburos. Despite promises to increase participation, the KRG encouraged a strong two-party system that excluded

13. The idea of a modern personality, informed by Max Weber's distinction between traditional and bureaucratic societies, is considered an essential attribute of modernity. Events are viewed as a process of cause and effect and not part of a fatalistic life in which humans have no part. A modern personality contrasts to the personality traits of the traditional world that explain events and processes in mythical and supernatural ways.

nonpartisan individuals or opposition groups. It was controlled by the KDP and PUK and left no possibilities for alternative avenues of political expression. The election law and the 7 percent quota disadvantaged small parties and independents from participating in government. For instance, in the 1992 election independent candidates received .05 percent of the total valid votes for seats. Although the majority of deputies in the KNA represented urban educated and professional classes, with only one tribal chief on the KDP list and two represented on the PUK list, the vast majority represented the KDP or PUK (Barzani 1995, 44). Ultimately, political institutions, processes, and outcomes in the Kurdistan Region remained linked to *wasta* and not meritocracy, which kept the judiciary, universities, government, and media grounded in personalities and party-based affiliations (Schlumberger 2000, 250).

Further, although the KRG was created as a decentralized political system, it remained highly centralized. Kurdish leaders consulted with their politburos, many of whom formed the presidential council; however, they remained outside and above the KRG, which further undermined the legitimacy and influence of parliamentary rule. The KRG also was without a constitution, despite the efforts of Iraqi Kurdish lawyers to create a framework based on European legal principles. In fact, the proposed constitution for the Kurdistan Region was rejected by traditional leaders from the outset, allowing charismatic personalities to shape sociopolitical and economic affairs and not the rule of law. Moreover, the leadership and power-sharing issues remained unresolved. Even though election laws mandated another election to be held to select one leader of the Kurdistan Region, Barzani and Talabani retained dual leadership positions.[14]

Neo-patrimonial politics ultimately obstructed the effective implementation of relief programs and potential private sector initiatives. The KRG and its political parties prevented entrepreneurship by forcing farmers to sell their

---

14. Interviews with Jawer Namik, speaker of the KNA; Dr. Rosch Shawais, KRG minister of interior; Mohammed Towfiq, KRG minister of humanitarian aid and cooperation; and Hussein Sinjari, KRG deputy minister of reconstruction and development, Arbil, July 1992 and Mar. 1993. In these interviews there was a general difference of opinion along party lines regarding the leadership issue. The KDP wanted another election. The PUK claimed that with a constitutional government a president was unnecessary, and instead, supported a leader of the "Kurdistan Liberation Movement."

crops to the government, closing shops in the bazaar that sold wheat products above market prices, and confiscating unsold raw materials from individual merchants. By 1993, the Galala company, one of several Kurdish raw materials businesses that traded with central and southern Iraq, had to close its business because of high KRG-imposed taxes on marble extracts.[15] Private entrepreneurship also was discouraged by the KRG's failure to impose a system of individual property rights, even after it had assumed ownership of *miri* lands in the northern region in 1992. Instead, the KRG continued to apply Iraqi legislation to the Kurdistan Region (except for security rules against the Kurds) so that farmers could only lease land for given, but renewable, time periods. In some localities Kurdish officials even refused land leases because special regulations of Iraqi law allocated particular tracts of land to members of the Revolutionary Command Council (RCC).

If local politics impeded the effective delivery of aid, the early relief program made no effort to break down traditional social structures, weaken Ba'athist legacies, dismantle the Iraqi regime's centralized economy, or encourage conflict resolution strategies at the local level. Even after refugees had been resettled and the region relatively stabilized, donors and INGOs did not implement income generation, structural reform, or sustainable development projects that could have encouraged capacity building. When Dohuk governorate lost its electricity in August 1993, U.S. military engineer corps (Prime BEEF) and UN specialists did not repair the electrical grid or create an independent source of power in the region. Rather, they purchased and distributed generators that provided temporary but costly power dependent upon imported diesel. The European Community Humanitarian Office (ECHO), in coordination with Kurdish engineers, funded a project to repair the Darbandikan dam. This effort, however, ceased

---

15. Interview with Awat Barzinji, Arbil, Jan. 23, 2008. For example, in 1991 the Galala Company made an agreement with KRG officials to pay a tax of 50 ISD per MT, or seventy-five marble slabs. By March 1992 the KRG increased taxes to 220 ISD. Most of the marble factories in the Kurdistan Region could produce about 2,500 MT daily and consume 500 MT for the region, with a reserve of 2,000 MT. At the end of the year the Galala Company had 10,000 tons of marble to transport to its largest factory in Ramadi, but the KRG would not permit it and assumed the unsold marble. Quarry businesses reacted by forming a union, but eventually had to close operations because of the excessively high costs.

7. Car barge at Qandil, Dohuk governorate, ca. 1993. Photograph courtesy of Simon O'Keefe.

because of the politically charged nature of resources in Iraq, concern about stimulating Kurdish autonomy, and increasing Kurdish leverage in the country.[16]

The costs of nonrecognition prevented the KRG from acquiring foreign currency earnings or importing necessary capital goods, machinery, and spare parts that could have encouraged manufacturing, repaired industries, and supported self-sustainability. Programs to stimulate the agrarian economy, including the resettlement of Kurds to their original villages, did not involve mechanization or industrialization processes that could have created a regional market for agricultural products. Although the UNDP managed the industrial sector, by 1996 it still had no office in the Kurdistan Region to coordinate or work on industrial issues. The only two cement factories in the Kurdistan Region (Serchinar and Tasluja) ceased functioning or operated at partial capacity. Wheat silos, flour

16. The concern was that by changing the irrigation-based lakes into lakes providing electricity, the south and central regions would experience agricultural problems during the dry season and give the Kurdistan Region too much autonomy and control of power in the rest of the country.

mills, and local businesses remained in disrepair. The Suleymaniya cigarette factory increased production from 1,200 to 144,000 packs from 1991 to 1997; however, it functioned at partial capacity and had no access to official international markets for sales (Hussain 2000, 183–91). In fact, by 1993 only 5 percent of private industry was functioning, leaving key sectors such as construction, textiles, food production, and steel at a standstill.[17] Without the ability to implement its own tax-generating projects, adopt institution-building practices and training programs, acquire capital or foreign exchange, or negotiate with foreign governments to attract investments, the regional economy experienced no real structural change.[18]

Yet if structural constraints and institutional weakness hinder development, why did new income-generating activities such as petroleum smuggling thrive in the Kurdistan Region? Whereas during the prewar period Zakho and the border region were military outposts closed to commercial activities, after the Gulf War they became an essential source of income generation. Taxation and customs revenues generated by illicit trade at the Iraqi Kurdish–Turkish border earned approximately $750 million annually, providing the KRG in Arbil with about 85 percent of its revenues (Natali 1999; Stansfield 2003a). Smuggling also became active at Iraqi Kurdish–Iranian border points, particularly in livestock, tires, and equipment.

The early aid program may not have created the underground economy in the emergent Kurdish quasi-state, but it reinforced the need for it. Whereas during the prewar period the Kurdistan Region acted as conduit for goods entering and leaving Iraq, allowing some private entrepreneurs and localities to benefit from commercial transactions, during the early relief period it was subjected to a double sanctions regime that closed off legal routes to the rest of Iraq and

17. Interview with department manager and trader, Arbil, Chamber of Commerce and Industry, Ministry of Economics and Finance, Jan. 1994.

18. Interview with Dr. Zeki Fattah, economic advisor to the KRG, Council of Ministers, Arbil, Oct. 26, 2005. During this period there was enough investment to assure employment but not to raise per capita income. For real economic growth, the KRG would have needed to save about 70 percent of its revenues. With an annual population growth of 100,000 and a 5:1 dollar-to-worker ratio, the KRG would have needed about US$200 million for investment alone, which, instead, was absorbed by the population increases.

the region. These restrictions kept the Kurdistan Region disconnected from the regional and global economies. They also prevented it from engaging in international trade or establishing a much-needed modern transportation or communications network.

In this political-economic context, the external aid program discouraged legal business while encouraging illegal activities. Financial benefits emerged linked to extracting and redistributing resources (Kolsto 2006, 729; King 2001, 528). Kurdish entrepreneurs helped create and support parallel economies by controlling currencies, goods, and services passing through the region via the humanitarian program (Kopp 1996, 430). During the early postwar period, which was marked by a fragmentation of territory, the closing of major transportation routes, and reopening of other access roads, relief aid had a major impact on the Kurdish political economy by creating price differentials between zones and new profits for entrepreneurs tied to the KDP and PUK.[19] The main source of business exchanges shifted from Mosul to Zakho at the Turkish border, which benefited Dohuk governorate. Transportation routes from Mersin in southeastern Turkey became an important transit route to the Kurdistan Region, where a lucrative petroleum smuggling industry had emerged.[20] In 1991–93 Turkish border guards loosely interpreted border regulations and permitted truck drivers to keep tanks as large as 4,000 liters underneath their trucks to store smuggled fuel exports. Truck drivers earned up to US$5,000 on a good five-day journey from southeastern Turkey to refineries in Mosul or Kirkuk.

The positive externalities of aid also encouraged Kurdish officials to seek alternative ways to generate income and keep the economy afloat. Instead of arranging a revenue-sharing system between party-controlled regions, they imposed taxes on goods shipped within and across the green line, up to 15 percent of their total

---

19. Before the Gulf War, open transportation routes facilitated a more equal distribution of resources in the Kurdistan Region via two main roads, the Mosul road and the "back road" (the Atrush road). After 1991 the Mosul road was either closed or too insecure for humanitarian relief and commercial traffic, requiring drivers to use the longer Atrush road as the main thoroughfare between the oil refineries in central Iraq, the Kurdish governorates, and the Turkish border. The change in routes shifted influence and commercial traffic to the KDP-controlled Dohuk governorate.

20. Barzinji interview, Jan. 23, 2008.

value. Transporters had to pay a double tax, one for entering Iraqi Kurdistan and another for crossing governorates within the region. Some Kurdish elites circumvented aid conditionalities and benefited personally. They affiliated local NGOs with the ministries and created "silo taxes" for the wheat buy-back program. Tribal and political leaders, as well as contractors linked to INGOs and the political parties, used aid to their advantage by securing lucrative contracts in their regions and reaping financial benefits (Graham-Brown 1999, 236; Leezenberg 1999).

In this closed, underdeveloped, centralized economy, where loyalties to the traditional elite and their political parties remained salient, the aid program had the unintended consequence of encouraging conflict. It created its own subindustries that altered salary structures by creating wage differentials (Özerdem and Rufini 2005, 55). Living conditions varied with the disproportionate distribution of assistance within regions. Local nationals working for the UN made about two thousand dollars monthly, while the average teacher made less than twenty dollars. Socioeconomic distinctions started to emerge between the budding and affluent private entrepreneurs, high-level officials, UN-INGO employees, and local populations. Regional polarizations based on party alliances also led to competition for access to donor funds (Natali 1999).

Instead of trying to bridge existing cleavages between the Kurdish parties, donor agencies and foreign governments encouraged fragmentation. They treated Ma'soud Barzani and Jelal Talabani as individual party leaders and not part of a regional government. Some donors and INGOs favored particular parties and their affiliated regions, stirring jealousies at local levels. Within two years, the Kurdistan Region became mired in internecine warfare between the KDP and PUK, fracturing the KRG into two administrations in Arbil and Suleymaniya, respectively. Indeed, foreign governments and INGOs attempted to encourage an early termination of the civil war. Immediately after the outbreak of conflict between the KDP and PUK in 1994, international delegations visited the Kurdistan Region to encourage negotiation. The government of Turkey established a peacekeeping force in the Kurdistan Region, called the Peace Monitoring Force, to monitor the infighting between the KDP and PUK (Olson 2005, 33). Kurdish political party representatives also engaged in high-level meetings with U.S. officials abroad (Stansfield 2003a, 98). Despite international intervention, weak institutions, absence of the rule of law, and a culture of Kalashnikovs that tolerated violence hampered the noblest international efforts to engage in conflict resolution.

Isolation and Nonnegotiation

With a double-sanctions regime crippling the economy, traditional socio-political structures, monopolization of power by the two main parties, and limited international support, the emergent Kurdish quasi-state was too institutionally weak, economically underdeveloped, and politically disinterested to negotiate with the central government. Civil servants were often unpaid and food availability was limited. Most local populations lived in economic precariousness and depended upon the extended family system of diaspora remittances or sales of personal belongings to gain much-needed income. Where land was unmined and villages reconstructed, individuals traveled to the rural areas to seek temporary employment as seasonal workers, and then they returned to the city to sell their goods in the evening.

Nor was the Kurdish quasi-state encouraged to negotiate with Baghdad. In attempting to prevent the Saddamization of the Kurdish north, donor agencies, foreign governments, and INGOs unintentionally encouraged the notion of a Kurdistan Region apart from the Iraqi state and not membership in it. To be sure, the United States provided important political and financial support to the Iraqi National Congress (INC), led by Ahmed Chalabi, in the attempt to form a common Iraqi opposition movement comprising Kurds and Arabs alike. The INC maintained communications offices in the northern Kurdish town of Salahaddin and played a key role in mediating intraregional disputes, mainly between Kurds. Kurdish leaders participated in INC meetings with Shi'a and Sunni Arab opposition activists and shared information and security demands with the INC. At its eleventh party congress, the KDP emphasized its alliance with the INC by announcing a new program of "moderation, not maximalism," and autonomy within a federated Iraq. Still, the INC's objective was to overthrow Saddam Hussein, not to construct mechanisms of cooperation or integration between Kurds and Arabs or to convince Kurds that they were Iraqis first. The INC also had limited legitimacy among Kurds, which showed little support for Chalabi and remained tied to local power structures and, in particular, Barzani and Talabani. The INC influence significantly weakened after its failed attempt to overthrow Saddam Hussein in 1995 and withdrawal from the Kurdistan Region.

Instead of trying to bridge ethnic divisions between the regions, the external aid program reinforced them. The presence of a safe haven that legitimized aid to some parts of Iraq and not others created different opportunity structures for communities based on localities and political alliances. The "green line," or "militarized demarcation line" established by the U.N. in 1991, divided the Kurdistan Region nearly in half, as well as Baghdad-controlled territories from those under KRG control. It strengthened distinctions over the disputed lands—those territories claimed by the Kurds as part of Kurdistan but that remained south of the green line and under the administrative jurisdiction of Saddam Hussein. Because these territories, including Kirkuk province, were not considered part of the Kurdistan Region by INGOs and foreign governments, they were ineligible for foreign aid. Only those parts of Kirkuk that remained north of the green line, mainly in Chamchamal, could access humanitarian assistance, and even then, the Kurdish parties had their own biases against this region (Germian) as an Islamic stronghold and constrained aid allocations. These internal boundaries and the uneven aid distributions shaped around them elevated existing tensions between Arbil and Baghdad, as well as between the Kurdish parties, over determining the status of Kirkuk and the disputed territories.

Indeed, center-periphery relations were not entirely disrupted after 1992. Where economic opportunities were available, business relationships were sustained or developed between the Kurdistan Region and territories outside the green line, including Baghdad. Resource exchanges and commercial linkages, mainly in the form of smuggling, continued between Kurdish contractors and those in other parts of Iraq, despite the internal embargo. Kurdish trading companies tied to the INGO market had to receive an export permit from Baghdad to transport goods from central and southern Iraq through Mosul (Khrar/Fida checkpoint) to Arbil. This business arrangement was subject to sporadic border closing, price increases, and bribery; however, it was an important source of revenues for key sectors of the local Kurdish economy, namely transportation and the underground petroleum market and its related activities.

The smuggling economy that defined post–Gulf War Iraqi Kurdistan also was part of an emergent quasi-private sector dependent upon Baghdad and regional states (Gazdar and Hussain 2002, 56). The central government's withdrawal of subsidies to local populations and replacement with a rationing system, coexistence of different regional currencies, and increasing need for food items for the PDS in the southern and central regions encouraged new commercial ties between contractors based on bartering food and fuel and a new dollar-exchange market.[21] Private entrepreneurs became active in licensing and marketing food products and established commercial linkages with local trading companies, money exchangers, and Baghdad officials. They profited not only from the U.S. dollar market but from exchanges made between northern and southern IDs, Turkish liras, and Iranian toman. The food-for-fuel trade gave Baghdad much-needed food items while providing the Kurdistan Region with petroleum, cement, black oil, rebar, asphalt, and bitumen for construction projects, creating a commodities market for fuel.

Merchants and contractors in Baghdad also established "phantom companies" that traded petroleum and materials in behalf of the central government at a fraction of the prices demanded by regional markets, which benefited parts of the Kurdistan Region. These companies procured kerosene from Mosul and resold it to INGOs, local organizations, and individuals at a fraction of the price of petroleum from Turkey. Quasi-illegal trade at the Jordanian border, which was subjected to a more flexible sanctions regime, allowed Kurdish war profiteers to import cheap products and continue their business activities with merchants in southern and central parts of the country.

The KRG also made deals with Baghdad and regional states to keep the administration alive. As in the prewar period, the unequal distribution of resources demanded negotiations between regions. Although the Kurds dismantled the power lines linking the dams in the north to the Iraqi electrical grid, communications continued with electricity control stations in the south. The KRG continued to provide water for irrigation needs in southern and central Iraq that often left the Kurdistan Region short of its water requirements. Dohuk governorate eventually turned to Turkey to source its energy demands temporarily; however, electricity was not channeled to the KRG but to the Mosul governorate via Zakho and then back to Dohuk. This arrangement left the Dohuk governorate dependent for power upon the Mosul Dam, which was controlled by the central government. Further, some high-ranking Kurdish party members continued to work for the Iraqi secret service (*mukhabarat*), which maintained an office near to the Kurdistan Parliament building in Arbil. The KDP even

21. For example, one box of cigarettes in Abidjan costs US$1, while in Zakho it cost nearly nothing. American cigarettes that entered Iraq via Jordan benefited the Kurdistan Region because Kurdish traders re-exported them to Turkey at an important profit.

established a temporary alliance with Saddam Hussein in 1996 to help expel the PUK from Arbil.

Similarly, to maintain an open border and reap the benefits of lucrative customs taxes, the KRG established security agreements with the Turkish government, which included shared efforts to search for PKK activists in the border area. A triangular relationship emerged among Iraqi Kurdish political parties, the Turkish government, and the PKK that led to renewed internal conflicts between Kurdish parties. The KRG also established political relations with Iran and Syria and maintained offices for its political parties in Iranian Kurdish border areas, Damascus, and the Syrian border region at Feshkabor. The nonofficial link at Feshkabor facilitated travel of government delegations, INGO workers, and individuals to the Kurdistan Region when the Turkish border was closed.

Still, as in the prewar period, these political deals and commercial exchanges did not positively affect the vast majority of populations in the Kurdistan Region. Although the KRG received about US$750 million annually from taxation at the Iraqi-Kurdish-Turkish border, most of the revenues benefited individuals tied to the KDP or PUK, private companies linked to the state, and privileged entrepreneurs in particular regions (Gazdar and Hussain 2002, 40). Two of the largest four companies in the food and fuel trading industry belonged to relatives of Saddam Hussein and were located in Kirkuk and Mosul. In Arbil and Dohuk only a few companies acquired contracts and most were unable to access the public sector. Absence of systemic revenue or power-sharing processes prevented the emergence of regional interdependencies and more integrated local economies that could have encouraged cooperation.

Closed economies and unresolved political issues undermined negotiation between the Kurdistan Region and Baghdad. During the first nine months after the Gulf War a delegation of representatives from the KF attempted to reach a compromise with Baghdad over Kurdish autonomy; however, negotiations ultimately terminated over Kirkuk. Ongoing policies of Arabization, an environment of fear instilled by Saddam Hussein, and heightened political awareness of the Anfal genocide reinforced the distrust that existed between most Kurds and Baghdad. As the political economy stagnated in the Kurdistan Region and deteriorated in the rest of Iraq, daily contacts between populations became difficult to sustain. Indeed, where education and employment opportunities were available cultural and social interactions continued across regions. Kurdish populations living in territories outside the green line, including Christian communities, liaised with Arabic-speaking Christians in Mosul and Baghdad, just as they did in the prewar period.

After 1994, however, it was increasingly dangerous for Kurds to conduct business in Baghdad or to interact with merchants outside the region. Although the Galala Company traded with central and southern Iraq, most of fourteen marble slab factory owners in the Kurdistan Region refused to export marble stones to Baghdad. Similarly, middle-class families no longer had the income or personal security to travel to central or southern Iraq or to other neighboring Arab countries. Over time, forced isolation turned into voluntary isolation, limiting interactions between communities and creating notions of territorial and political separation based on ethnicity and territory.

Conclusions

The first relief period in the Kurdistan Region assured the immediate needs of local populations affected by the Persian Gulf War. It provided the stimulus for recovery, rehabilitation, and resettlement of local populations. These development processes encouraged the semi-legitimacy of the KRG and supported the idea of a Kurdish quasi-state apart from Iraq. Yet the limited and short-term nature of the aid program, intertwined with domestic structural constraints, prevented much-needed reforms that could have supported Kurdish self-sustainability. Instead of an autonomous Kurdistan Region, what emerged was a partially legitimized territory of Iraq that was highly dependent upon external patronage for its survival. Ongoing marginalization of the KRG and authoritarianism in Baghdad also hindered any potential relationship from developing with the central government outside underground economies and political conflict.

3

From Relief to Rehabilitation

ALTHOUGH THE U.S.-FUNDED RELIEF PROGRAM ended in 1996, external aid to the Kurdistan Region continued under the OFFP. Ongoing assistance provided the necessary external patronage and international support to help keep the Kurdish quasi-state alive, as well as to encourage political stability, institution building, and new forms of revenue generation. Over time, the aid program engaged in reconstruction and attempted to develop industries and local infrastructure. More expansive trade emerged within the region and across borders that generated new forms of wealth. Even then, the OFFP, like the first relief program, supported the territorial integrity of Iraq and not the self-sustainability of the Kurdistan Region. It remained committed to the one-Iraq policy, which hindered capacity building and kept the region isolated, underdeveloped, and without internal sovereignty in the Iraqi state. In the absence of official commercial transactions and with continued authoritarian rule in Baghdad, no positive relationship could develop between the KRG and the central government. The ties that emerged across regions were largely based on tutelage and toleration, without any mechanisms of mutual support or integration.

The OFFP Period

Like the first relief phase, the OFFP provided the Kurdish quasi-state with important services and revenues that alleviated the immediate effects of the double embargo and permitted economy recovery. The OFFP was an agreement or compromise made by the UN sanctions committee in New York that permitted the Iraqi government to sell increasing but limited amounts of petroleum for food and humanitarian needs of civilian populations. Under the program, which was implemented in thirteen six-month phases, the northern region—territories above the U.N. demarcation line—was targeted to receive 13 percent of the proceeds of Iraqi oil sales for humanitarian goods (Graham-Brown 1999, 275–77).

As in the first aid period, the program placed particular attention on the special rehabilitation needs of the three northern governorates. Although the OFFP allocated 59 percent of its revenues to central and southern Iraq, the cash component provided 35 percent more per capita to the Kurdish north than to the rest of the country. UNICEF, for instance, had its largest budget and highest annual procurement in the northern region (UNICEF 1998; UNICEF 2002, 16; FAO 2002, 1). The program also permitted ongoing security assistance. The U.S. government terminated its humanitarian relief support in August 1996 but assured ongoing security protection to the Kurds by transitioning OPC II to Operation Northern Watch.

The difference, however, was in the nature and scope of the OFFP. In contrast to the first relief phase, whereby donor agencies and foreign governments had limited political engagement with the KRG and its rival parties, after 1996 external actors became increasingly involved in stabilizing the Kurdish north as a means of checking the influence of Saddam Hussein. In support of ongoing efforts by Kurdish officials and under the guidelines set by the Ankara peace process, the U.S. government brokered the Washington Agreement in September 1998 that officially terminated the Kurdish civil war (Stansfield 2003a, 100). Tensions remained between the parties; however, the agreement helped create the conditions of relative stability by officially dividing the KRG into two administrations controlled by the KDP and PUK in Arbil and Suleymaniya governorates, respectively. Even after the civil war ended, UN officials negotiated ongoing disputes between the parties and quelled potential conflicts. They taught principles of good governance, negotiation, and administration by conducting regular meetings with KRG representatives and incorporating local personnel into legitimate bodies. KRG representatives and local populations that liaised with the UN gained professional experience and language skills, while learning about the policies and protocols of international organizations.

In contrast to the first relief phase, whereby resources were insufficient to address local needs, the OFFP had excess money chasing needs. Aid revenues and services allocated to the Kurdistan Region increased exponentially, from 1 billion during the first relief program to nearly US$10 billion during the OFFP. Approximately US$29 million was initially targeted to the Kurdistan Region, with the first shipment commencing in March 1997.[1] The region also was allocated the interest on unspent funds of oil sale proceeds and gains on currency exchange. From this amount revenues were allocated to different sectors, the majority of which centered on food and medicines, but which also included agriculture, education, water and sanitation, de-mining, and electricity (Natali 2007c).

Indeed, the OFFP was corrupt and incomplete.[2] Only 51 percent, or US$14.7 million of the total initial allocation to the Kurdistan Region was received during the six-year period. The other 49 percent remained in a French bank, accruing interest at the profit of Saddam Hussein, the United Nations, and private entrepreneurs. The medical field, one of the OFFP's key targeted sectors, had an even lower allocation rate. By August 2002, of the total value of medicines allocated to the Kurdistan Region from the 13 percent account, only 29 percent was actually delivered. When the program terminated in November 2003, about US$3.7 billion remained in unspent funds.[3] Still, although the UN failed to provide the Kurdistan Region with its full 13 percent, it spent between US$4.1 and $6.1 billion worth of humanitarian goods in the north. The massive infusion of external aid allowed local populations to access food items that they otherwise could not have afforded, encouraged ongoing reconstruction, and helped improve the overall economic situation. More than half of UNICEF's budget was allocated to water and sanitation, which included distributing pumps, installing generators, and providing safe drinking water to local populations (UNICEF 1999, 3; Mahdi 2002, 22).

Like the earlier program, the OFFP also targeted local agriculture capabilities, and in some areas production improved. In the Deşti region of Hariri in Arbil province, for instance, where the Food and Agricultural Organization

1. Interview with Stafford Clarry, humanitarian affairs advisor to the KRG, Arbil, Nov. 2005. Clarry compiled the allocation/expenditure figure from UN sources.

2. For a detailed examination of the corruption involved in the OFFP see Volcker, Goldstone, and Pieth (2005, 3:149–62).

3. Interview with Stafford Clarry, Arbil, Oct.–Nov. 2005. Of the eleven six-month phases that were implemented, about US$346 million was allocated for Arbil (34 percent), Dohuk (23 percent), and Suleymaniya (43 percent) for the procurement, by the Iraqi central government, of medicines, medical supplies, and laboratory reagents. The final figure for unspent interest and gains on currency exchange is unavailable.

(FAO) planted grains and distributed machinery, local production increased to one thousand tons of rice and barley annually (FAO 2002). The OFFP vaccination program in Suleymaniya and parts of Kirkuk governorate helped raise the number of animals for husbandry by about 270 percent in 1997–99, alongside imports from neighboring states. The overall number of chicken farms in the region increased from 30 to 176, improving production capacity from 200,000 to 1,540,000 chickens annually. Increases in animal production led to decreases in the price of meat for local consumption (Hussain 2000, 135).[4]

The OFFP also encouraged economic change. The massive injection of funds altered exchange rates, influenced wages, and affected daily lives. To be sure, the ongoing UN sanctions regime prevented the legal export and import of goods and kept the Kurdistan Region dependent upon cross-border smuggling as a main source of income, just as it did during the first relief period. Sanctions strengthened the business of bartering food for fuel and supported the emergence of backstreet industries such as tank construction, restaurants, and parking lots for trucks smuggling oil and food.

Yet, as the magnitude of the OFFP increased, so too did the positive externalities of aid. The Kurdistan Region became a "free zone" for Iranian businesses that paid lower customs taxes at the unofficial checkpoint at Ibrahim Khalil (Habur) than at the official Iranian border points in the Persian Gulf. Kurdish entrepreneurs benefited by transferring their activities overseas and creating transportation businesses in the region. Goods from Dubai were reshipped into Kurdistan via Saudi Arabia, Jordan, Syria, and Turkey. Iraqi Kurds established dealerships with the Gulf States, Mersin, and China, and imported diverse food items from outside the region: bananas from Latin America, tea from Ceylon, and rice and food products from Asia. These transactions created the beginnings of a free market, although still shaped by an underground economy that was essentially import-driven. By 2000 exports increased by about 175 percent alongside general price increases. Total exports declined, however, while illegal imports of cars, spare parts, and clothes increased (Sliman 2002, 142).[5]

4. In 1994–99 prices decreased from 75 to 35 ISD for one kilo of mutton and 100 to 40 dinar per kilo of beef.

5. This increase is based on variable prices. The increase during the same period based on fixed prices, using 1996 as a base year, is about 147 percent.

In contrast to the first aid period, whereby short-term relief left the Kurdish quasi-state entirely dependent upon international donors and the underground economy, the OFFP partially and gradually permitted alternative and legal avenues for income generation. Although the OFFP did not create a private sector, the UN-directed business of distributing food, fuel, and humanitarian relief items created opportunities for an entrepreneurial class that became the impetus for private-sector contracting activities. It encouraged the creation of NGOs and contractors that acted as an implementing hand for the UN. Even though items for large contracts were procured outside Iraq, the UN used local companies to transport goods and equipment throughout the country. Unlike the private sector that emerged in the prewar period, however, the commercial activities that developed during the OFFP period were of a much larger magnitude. OFFP contracts and subcontracts were valued in the millions of dollars, which was more than what the Iraqi government ever permitted its contractors to manage.[6]

The revival of the semiofficial trade sector reinvigorated stagnant chambers of commerce and created an environment in which people had the resources and sense of security to engage in business.[7] From 1995 to 2000 small businesses for food industrial projects in the Kurdistan Region increased from 60 to 169, while the total number of small industrial projects in the region, excluding Kirkuk, reached 608. All these factories except two belonged to the private sector (Barwari 2002). Emergent private-sector activities had their greatest impact in the construction and trade arenas, which were redefined by UN contracting procedures requiring an open bidding process. These procedures, while overly bureaucratic, encouraged the standardization of tendering activities and a more diverse and competitive market. For instance, the UN housing agency, HABITAT, spurred internal trading in the Kurdish construction market, strengthened capacities to penetrate local markets, and provided jobs for

6. Interview with Bahzad H. Akirawy, administrative manager, Kurdistan Contractor's Union, Arbil, Mar. 5, 2006.

7. Interview with Hassan Baqi Hawrami, chairman, Suleymaniya Chamber of Commerce, Suleymaniya, Dec. 3, 2007. The Suleymaniya Chamber of Commerce was established in 1967 but was virtually inactive since then, even during first relief period. It became active after 2003.

TABLE 2. NUMBER OF SMALL DOMESTIC INDUSTRIAL FACTORIES IN SULEYMANIYA GOVERNORATE, 1990–2001.

Year	Food industry	Paper and wood industry	Quality assurance industry	Chemical and plastics industry	Textile industry	Maintenance and services	Metal industry	Total
1990	7	1	10	0	2	6	0	26
1991	9	1	9	0	1	6	1	27
1992	8	1	8	0	4	8	1	30
1993	7	1	7	2	2	8	1	28
1994	7	1	5	1	4	9	0	27
1995	6	1	5	2	8	3	0	25
1996	7	1	7	4	6	1	4	30
1997	9	1	8	2	0	1	1	22
1998	6	0	14	1	0	1	4	26
1999	15	0	25	0	0	3	4	47
2000	39	0	59	0	0	14	7	119
2001	9	11	62	0	5	11	9	107
Total	129	19	219	12	32	71	32	514

Source: Documents from the Chamber of Commerce and Industry and the Directorate of Assistance to the Ministry of Industry and Energy, Suleymaniya Governorate, 2002.

skilled and unskilled laborers. The sheer size and number of projects created opportunities for laborers, engineers, and masons to win small contracts in the towns and villages.

One of the unintended consequences of the OFFP was an exponential increase in personal wealth for local entrepreneurs. Businessmen benefited by holding crude-oil contracts, altering their "NGO" activities to meet UN transportation needs, or establishing joint ventures to accommodate the business of transporting food, medicines, and cement from factories in southern Iraq, Turkey, Iran, and the Kurdistan Region in exchange for diesel. Others traveled to Mersin in Turkey and purchased goods in U.S. dollars, which were then sold to markets in Iraqi Kurdistan in the local currency at considerable profit.

The infusion of cash into the Kurdish economy advantaged those engaged in money exchanges, buying and smuggling petroleum and cigarettes to Turkey, or selling equipment to Iran, despite exchange-rate fluctuations and the depreciation of the ISD by over 80 percent.[8] It also led to an increase in daily wages, particularly for those trading in U.S. dollars. Consequently, some people became very rich. Whereas during the first relief period aid profits were largely confined to the two main political parties, the OFFP helped create a more expansive class of wealthy merchants that included tribal leaders and political officials. This class of nouveaux riche became prominent apart from the traditional families, although they were still influenced by the Kurdish parties.

Greater avenues for wealth generation, alongside international supervision of potential political disputes, encouraged relatively stable governance. Instead of competing for power in Arbil, the two Kurdish administrations focused on governorate-level development by creating municipalities and local agencies. Education departments established new courses for civic society and human rights that were integrated into primary and secondary school programs. The two regional administrations also had more revenues to reinvest locally. In conjunction with publicly owned and produced activities such as rented land and factories, the KRG in Arbil earned about US$1.5–2.5 billion in 1992–2003, with per capita government spending of about US$100–150 per person annually. Public expenditures included purchases of lands, houses, and livestock; provision of free education, healthcare, security, water, and electricity; and road construction and other social welfare services.[9]

Economic changes gave rise to more expansive areas of sociopolitical organization and participation. The KRG's new tax rate on OFFP-related projects increased competition and caused rising costs of materials and contracts, which encouraged the emergence of syndicates and trade unions. Already disadvantaged by the depreciation of the ISD, Kurdish contractors created the Kurdistan Contractors Union (KCU) in 2001 in all three governorates to support private-

8. Prior to the OFFP the exchange rate was about US$1 = 90 ISD. After 1997 it changed from US$1 = 20 ISD, and then to US$1 = 10 ISD. The tobacco-smuggling industry is based in Cyprus, where cigarettes are produced cheaply and then shipped to the Kurdistan Region via Turkey. One carton sells for about US$400 in Iraqi Kurdistan. It is then resent from the Zakho border back to Turkey and resold for about US$600 per carton.

9. Fattah interview. It is important to note that each KRG administration (Arbil-Dohuk and Suleymaniya) established different policies, civil codes, public offices, and ministries to manage political and economic development issues within its respective governorate.

sector initiatives. The KCU aimed to lower taxes for union members, represent the unions in dispute over contracts, protect workers and businesses, lobby the KRG to lower its tax rate, and assist private individuals in establishing their business needs.[10] Some health conditions also ameliorated during this period. By 1999 the rate of fully immunized children increased from about 24 to 42 percent, while child mortality declined to the lowest rates in the entire country, from 90 to 72 per thousand births (Graham-Brown 2002, 283; Stansfield 2003b, 134; UNICEF 1999, 3–4).

Maintaining the Status Quo

With the vast amount of resources made available by the OFFP, willing aid recipients, and relatively stable administrations in the provinces, one would have expected a self-sustainable Kurdish quasi-state. By 2001 the international sanctions regime had been renegotiated, which gave the Iraqi government the right to sell its petroleum and increased allocations of humanitarian goods and services. OFFP revenues for the Kurdistan Region increased from US$260 million biannually during the first four plans to US$4 billion, providing the Kurds with about US$520 million every six months thereafter.[11] Yet, despite increased revenues and more expansive economic activities, no real structural changes occurred in the Kurdish political economy during this period.

Like the first relief program, the OFFP remained committed to the sovereignty regime and the one-Iraq policy. It treated the autonomous Kurdistan Region as part of the Iraqi state and required it to follow the same rules and procedures as provinces below the green line under the rule of Saddam Hussein. Despite the weakening of the sanctions regime, the main tenet remained in place: no goods or products could be imported or exported from Iraq, including oil. The OFFP also was bound to strict procurement rules and conditionalities made by

10. Khaffaf interview; Akirawy interview; interview with Abdul Aziz, Kurdistan Contractors Union of Dohuk, Dohuk, May 11, 2006. The first women's syndicate and youth union were created in 1953, however, the contractor's union did not become active until after 2003 as a means of protecting workers and businesses. In 2006, the Arbil Contractors Union had 511 members between trading, construction, and transportation sectors.

11. Clarry interview, Nov. 2005. Arbil, and compiled UN documents.

the sanctions committee in New York, which retained ultimate decision-making authority on the distribution of monies and projects upon which the OFFP's six-month funding cycles were based.[12] The committee devised a special list of goods that were permitted to enter Iraq sporadically, while refusing or holding "dual-purpose" items that could be used for industrial or military purposes.[13] Most nonfood and nonmedical items were prohibited from entering the country.

Exceptions were eventually made for the OFFP program with Jordan; however, the UN prohibited goods from being purchased inside the Kurdistan Region (Mahdi 2002, 21; Kirk and Sawdon 2002, 7; Graham-Brown 1999, 72, 186, 311; UNICEF 2002, 33–34). Even sand and gravel were brought in from outside the country. Nor could the UN or aid recipients support Kurdish civil servants employed by the KRG and disconnected from Ba'athist regime. The rationale was that local procurement or employment, even if made in the Kurdistan Region, could support Saddam Hussein and the Iraqi government.

The ongoing commitment to Iraqi sovereignty assured the minimum humanitarian needs of local populations but not rehabilitation of the infrastructure. The initial phases of the OFFP essentially replicated the first relief period, although food and fuel distributions were conducted on a larger scale. Over 50 percent of the OFFP budget was used to provide supplies (UNICEF 2002, 31). Aid allocations increased over time; however, the KRG still could not purchase the necessary equipment to make investments, build technology, stir local production, engage in legal import-export activities, or develop taxation programs.[14] In fact, there was even resistance to capacity-building by foreign donors, and regional governments worried about a rising autonomous Kurdistan.

To be sure, in October 2000 the UN introduced a new country program that moved beyond physical rehabilitation of the infrastructure to quality of services

12. Interview with Maxwell Gaylard, former coordinator of the OFFP for the northern region and current United Nations Mine Action Service, Department of Peacekeeping Operations, New York, Sept. 7, 2006.

13. Barzinji interview, Jan. 13, 2007. Dual-purpose items included truck tires and pencils. The concern by the sanctions committee was that ten billion pencils could produce a low percentage of pure graphite, which could create an atomic reactor.

14. Interview with Douglas Layton, director, Kurdistan Development Corporation, Arbil, Sept. 27, 2005.

and social sector planning (UNICEF 1999, 2). The FAO no longer emphasized short-term delivery of basic agriculture inputs, but rather, medium-term projects such as rehabilitating the agricultural sector to include food-processing industries. UNICEF attempted capacity-building measures at the governorate and district levels by implementing nutrition programs in Arbil, training health-care personnel, and distributing medicines, supplies, and essential equipment. It established partnerships with over thirty local NGOs in the region to implement water and sanitation projects (UNICEF 1998, 39; UNICEF 2000, 43; UNICEF 2002, 20; FAO 2002, 1). In 1997–98 UNICEF efforts helped increase enrollment rates in primary and intermediate schools in the Kurdistan Region by 25 percent.

Still, like the first relief program, the OFFP failed to implement capacity-building projects that would underpin long-term development and growth. It did not alter its major conditionalities, six-month planning cycles, or limitations on the use of cash as a means of encouraging self-sustainability. Even after the increase in oil prices, skyrocketing of program budgets, passing of UNSCR 1409, and pressures to shift the focus from relief to rehabilitation, the UN rejected capacity building. FAO's warnings about the negative impact of importing wheat on local production went unheeded by the UN sanctions committee, despite the fact that U.S. Food for Peace regulations prohibited the export of surplus wheat to agriculturally fertile lands and U.S. government representatives had an important voice on the committee.

OFFP conditionalities discouraged a self-sufficient agricultural sector. In contrast to the first relief period, whereby the aid program encouraged farmers to plant through a local wheat-purchase scheme, the OFFP involved a massive infusion of food aid that undermined local capacities, deflated prices, and further weakened the productive elements of society (Billet 1993, 22–23). Rather than purchasing 500,000 MT of wheat grown in the Kurdistan Region from local farmers, which could have supplied part of the 700,000 MT needed for the monthly food basket (PDS), the OFFP purchased wheat from Australia, spending half of procurement costs on transportation (Natali 2007c, 1119; FAO 2002, 7). Similarly, instead of restoring local grain facilities, building much needed silos, or repairing the numerous flour mills in the Kurdistan Region, the OFFP tried to obtain "economies of scale" by procuring food items in behalf of Baghdad and sending them to warehouses in Kirkuk and Mosul, whereby the food was then distributed by the WFP in conjunction with food departments in the Kurdistan Region.[15] Kurdish food agents played an important role in the distribution process, yet the overall program in the north remained in the control of the UN-Baghdad and not the KRG. Excess availability of imported food led to a decline in the prices of local agricultural goods, the switching of crops (from wheat to barley), and reduction in the acreage of planting, which caused an overall decline in wheat production (Hussain 2000, 23).[16] From 1995 to 1999 wheat productivity decreased by 68 percent, from approximately 665,000 to 112,000 MT, followed by additional years of sporadic production levels. Indeed, three continuous years of drought and decrease in the product value of wheat in 1997–2002 contributed to the decline in local production levels (FAO 2002, 1, 55).

Yet, even after the drought years, the costs of planting and cultivating wheat increased with greater dependency on tractors, water wells, and pumps that required electricity and gasoline. With high production costs, low prices caused by the WFP food basket, sanctions restrictions on trade, and small inefficient plots (20-donum average), many Kurdish farmers could not compete with the OFFP's subsidized food imports, and they abandoned their crops for UN food handouts. Others stopped planting summer crops, used their grain as livestock feed, or purchased wheat and other food products from Basra, Baghdad, and neighboring states. Consequently, although the Kurdish agriculture sector had previously served as an important source of state tax, by 2001 only 16 percent of the wheat crop was sold in local markets (FAO 2002, 13–14). Despite the KRG's efforts to compensate for limited silo capacity by putting up tents and plastic linings, local production was far below capacity.

The continued distribution of food aid also had a psychological impact on Kurdish society. It corrupted mentalities by weakening demand and incentives

15. Volcker, Goldstone, and Pieth (2005, 4:112–19).

16. Interview with Hamza Rasoul, Directorate of Agriculture, Arbil, Mar. 31, 2007. The price and yield of wheat crops also depends upon its variety. Kandaha, for instance, is high-quality wheat and is priced at about US$100 per donum. Determining the quality of wheat also requires an analysis for amino acid, which cannot be done in the Kurdistan Region without the necessary apparatus.

for cultivators to plant. Local populations benefited in the short term because the program ensured that everyone had food. Still, by supporting the WFP food ration system and later expanding it to include all individuals resident in Iraq, the OFFP entitled everyone to a ration regardless of need. Over time, consumer demand and living patterns changed so that upwardly mobile local populations living in urban centers were eating prepackaged foods. This system distorted markets and economic life while giving the central government greater control of the food supply (Kirk and Sawdon 2002, v). It reinforced the culture of dependency and people's expectations of the role of government based on the distribution of food and social services. Without equity follow-up, the OFFP strengthened the notion that had emerged during the Ba'athist social welfare state that people should receive goods and revenues without work. Many families sold their food rations in the market for cash, which provided short-term assistance but further weakened the work ethic of Kurdish society.

Certainly, as in the prewar and first relief periods, impediments to development were not solely due to foreign aid. Structural legacies remained present: underground economies, absence of capital, obsolete infrastructures, and weak institutional capacity (Chorev 2007, 62; UNICEF 1998, 39). Although the KRG implemented laws to encourage business, the local market was not open to private-sector growth. Industrial development was limited to small factories that employed only one or two workers and generally remained within the family. The Kurdish cash-bazaar economy still had no banking system to finance economic projects or supply loans, which left local entrepreneurs without revenues to invest. Many depended upon the traditional *hawlana* system for loans or turned to leading families or the parties as sources of financing, reinforcing the role of *wasta* in determining the allocation and distribution of resources.

Additionally, the market was never really separated from the government, but rather, remained in the shadow of the Kurdish quasi-state, that is, the KRGs and their political parties. Private entrepreneurs that received large contracts with the UN, generally established families or tribal leaders, were required to negotiate a portion of their profits or engage in "joint ventures" with the parties. Whereas small- to medium-scale construction projects diversified as part of a budding private sector, large-scale investments such as the telecommunica-

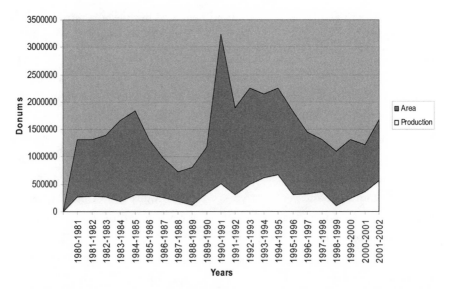

8. Cultivated area (in donums) and production of wheat (in MT) in the Kurdistan Region, 1980–2002. *Source:* FAO 2003.

tions sector, which remained outside the OFFP until 2002, were monopolized by influential families tied to the KDP and PUK.[17]

Neopatrimonial politics continued to impede political and economic reform. The two main political parties benefited from the externalities of aid, just as they did during the first relief period, by imposing internal taxes on goods transported within the region, which increased costs for merchants and populations in outlying areas. They also impeded effective aid delivery despite UN mediation efforts. Electricity shortages were as much a consequence of party infighting as they were a result of ineffective UN policies. For example, because the Darbandikan and Dokan dams were in territories "controlled" by the PUK, the issue of sharing water with the KDP, which had sided with Turkey during the three-month conflict in 1997, became highly politicized. Officials in Suleymaniya considered the dam "PUK water" and used it as leverage over Baghdad and the KDP, particularly during the drought years of 1998–99.

17. Korak Telecommunications won the contract to supply telecommunications in the Dohuk-Arbil region, with a sister company, Sana, in Suleymaniya. Asia Cell monopolizes the telecommunications sector in Suleymaniya.

9. Al-Sawaf Mosque in Arbil, ca. 2008. Photograph courtesy of Ali Ayverdi.

Instead of encouraging decentralization processes beyond the provincial level, the two administrations reinforced political party power inside the governorates. Decision making was not part of a more inclusive process involving the governors, newly created municipalities, or outlying regions. Rather, it remained consolidated in the party politburos. Power rivalries also became tied to emergent regionalisms that reinforced polarizations between political, linguistic, and cultural communities. For instance, Dohuk province, influenced by the KDP, established a separate study program for the Badini dialect in primary schools as a means of equalizing, differentiating, and elevating the governorate and its people from Sorani-speaking communities in Arbil and Suleymaniya. This effort underlined the growing influence of Barzani family–KDP power and the ongoing party competitions for power, resources, and leadership in the region.

The unsettled political climate constrained possibilities for long-term development, just as it did during the first relief period. Internal party competitions, tensions between Turkey, the PKK, and Iraqi Kurds, closure of the Turkish border in 1997 to INGO workers, intervention of Turkish military forces in Dohuk province, and the capture of PKK leader Abdullah (Apo) Ocalan in 1999 created new challenges to internal governance and impeded aid delivery to certain regions.

By 1998 the Kurdistan Region had 350,000 IDPs, half of which were women and children (UNICEF 1998, 6–10). Unstable conditions also allowed Islamic groups to gain influence in the region, which created new rivalries between the parties and regional states. Islamic groups solicited aid and offered generous social welfare assistance to local populations. In 1996–99, international organizations such as the World Assembly of Muslim Youth (WAMY) spent 13,835,094 ISD, or about US$700,000 on sixty-seven projects involving mosque construction and repair in the villages, towns, and cities of Dohuk and Arbil governorates (MWIA 2000). The Iranian government funded clinics along the border region and offered local Iraqi Kurdish doctors up to US$1,000 monthly in salaries.

The Kurdish parties also used Islamic groups to co-opt and control local populations. During and after the Kurdish civil war, for instance, the KRG-Arbil (KDP) appealed to moderate members of the IMK as a strategy for strengthening its power base. It invited an IMK representative to become minister of justice and charged the Ministry of Waqfs and Islamic Affairs (MWIA) to construct, repair, and manage mosques, Islamic schools, and institutions in the region. In 2000–2003 the MWIA allocated 1,672,367,200 OID, or about US$83.6 million, for mosque construction and repair in Arbil and Dohuk governorates (MWIA 2006).[18] Other groups radicalized. In reaction to the KRG-Arbil's attempt to control Islamic influences by closing of the "mosques in the evening" and placing them under the control of local security forces (asaysh), extremist IMK members splintered into small groups. These cells—al-Hamas (the battalion of Abu Abaydi al-Jahra), Jamiat Tawhid, Hezi Soran, and Junda Islam—became the precursors of Ansar al-Islam, which engaged in armed conflict with the Kurdish administrations and their political parties in the Iranian border regions.[19]

The time and resources allocated to these security issues, alongside the culture of secrecy tied to Ba'athist legacies, further limited KRG attention from

18. Interview with Adnan Naqshbandiyya, minister of Waqfs and Islamic Affairs, KRG, Arbil, Apr. 12, 2006. This figure does not include funding for houses for imams or Islamic schools. The condition of IMK participation in the KRG was that it severs ties with Iran, remains under the control of the KRG-Arbil (KDP), and abides by the rules of the Kurdistan Region.

19. Interview with an anonymous informant, Arbil, Apr. 17, 2006. The IMK responded to the KDP's co-optation efforts and did not defend the evening mosques like it did when the PUK was in control of Arbil, although extremists wanted them reopened.

engineering reform. By 2000 the region still lacked social capital and participatory organizations at the local levels (Fukayama 2002, 33–34). Most of 10,000 Kurds that were trained and worked with U.S.-funded programs during the first aid period had been evacuated to the United States, adding to the brain drain that had commenced in 1992 and leaving the region without qualified physicians, engineers, lawyers, and competent administrators. Despite the existence of farmers unions and associations in 64 percent of the villages in the Kurdistan Region, formal membership was between 4 and 18 percent (FAO 2002, 19).

Nor did the KRG have enforceable laws that required children to receive a primary education or protected women from domestic violence (UNICEF 2000, 9–10). Urbanization processes helped increase student populations in the cities; however, in the rural areas children were discouraged from continuing their studies after primary school. Further, honor killings and female genital mutilation remained rampant in the region. The KRG in Arbil may have passed an honor killing law in 2000 to impose harsher prison sentences and to treat honor killing as murder, but legal, institutional, and cultural constraints precluded the rule of law.[20] The highly centralized judicial system under the two KRG Ministries of Justice (MOJ) was not independent and lacked a constitutional court and uniform legal code. The Kurdistan Region also was still legally tied to the Iraqi judicial system and did not have the authority to change Iraqi laws, only to make amendments to it (JRI-KS 2006, 4). Moreover, traditional social norms rooted in tribal and customary laws often took precedence over the official penal code and allowed honor crimes to continue without punishment.

Still, like the first aid period, the OFFP offered no opportunities for the Kurdish quasi-state to engage in institutional change, increase service delivery capacity, or address long-term strategic needs. The ongoing sanctions regime prevented entrepreneurs from acquiring loans or implementing microfinance projects that could have established the necessary foundations for local business development and encouraged notions of trust and collateral through borrowing. Procurement conditionalities resulted in long delays in obtaining import permits

---

20. The 1969 law of the Iraqi penal code (art. 409) states that if a man kills one of the women in his family—either an aunt, sister, wife, or daughter—in a case of adultery, his action is treated as a crime. This crime, however, was considered as a "special case," which often left those complicit in the killing unpunished while failing to condone the crime itself.

from the Ministry of Foreign Affairs (MOFA) in Baghdad, even for shipments through the Zakho border (UNICEF 2002, 31). UN officials eventually introduced new contracting procedures and paved the way for professional standards; however, they awarded prime contracts without supervision or accountability. Nor did the OFFP attempt to break the culture of secrecy that defined the Iraqi information services. The UN often refused to release information about the PDS and educational and health-care sectors to Kurdish officials, arguing that it was the "property of the Iraqi government" (Benini 2005).

The UNDP, which is mandated to channel resources through host governments for development, made no attempt to implement self-sustainability and infrastructure projects and had no engagement with the KRG (Barakat and Chard 2005, 179). It did not commence activities in the Kurdistan Region until 2002, and even then, its programs fostered dependency by local populations. Like the first relief program, instead of developing an independent source of electricity, the UNDP purchased low-kVA generators for entire neighborhoods in the region, creating greater household reliance on fuel.[21] Although the Office of the United Nations High Commissioner for Refugees (UNHCR) employed low-cost, micro-quick-impact projects as part of its refugee assistance programs in other parts of the world, none was implemented in the Kurdistan Region (Zetter 2005, 162, 179). Similarly, in 1997–2003, the UN's International Telecommunications Unit allocated US$100 million to the Kurdistan Region but accomplished no concrete projects other than purchasing and installing digital exchanges from Iran. Industrialization projects were either partially implemented or failed outright. In one case the UN attempted to create six large factories for food production and marble. Absence of feasibility studies and an industrial policy for the Kurdistan Region, as well as inefficient procurement policies, resulted in the factories' closure within one year.[22]

21. For instance, had the OFFP developed the Bekhma dam for US$2 billion, the Kurdistan Region could have had 1,400 MGW of electricity. Instead it purchased four large generators at 9 MW each for Arbil city, costing US$2.5 million each and which ran on diesel that required 360 barrels per month per generator.

22. Interview with Azad A. Tutinçi, general director, KRG Ministry of Industry and Electricity, General Directorate of Industry, Arbil, Jan. 10, 2007. These efforts included two sunflower oil factories, a tomato paste factory in Harir, dairy products factories in Sumail and Suleymaniya and a

As the largest humanitarian aid program in the history of international aid, the OFFP certainly had enough money to engage in capacity and infrastructure-building projects. It could have paid the salaries for local teachers, many of whom were living below subsistence levels (at the end of the OFFP, teachers were still making less than twenty dollars monthly), developed training programs for civil servants, invested in operating systems, created a modern sewage system, closely monitored violence and killing of women, or initiated education reform. Specialized in bureaucratic procedures, the UN certainly had the technical expertise to replace the antiquated Ottoman administrative system in the region with a more modernized and standardized one. Yet it failed to engage in public sector administrative reform or training, which benefited the Kurdish elite by allowing personalities to shape political decisions and outcomes, rather than the rule of law.

The near-absence of capacity and infrastructure building also left the mechanism of life in the villages and towns underdeveloped. Schools were rebuilt without books, clinics were established without medicines or qualified physicians, and village houses were constructed without vital services such as electricity, access roads, and potable water.[23] Although some health conditions improved, high illiteracy rates continued, particularly in the rural areas. By 2002 about 68 percent of rural household members in the three Kurdish governorates were either illiterate or had an education less than primary school (FAO 2002, 4, 9, 21–24; Kirk and Sawdon 2002, 45). Low education levels, in turn, hampered the possibility of improving agricultural productivity by replacing traditional methods with modern technologies. Agriculture remained based on subsistence and not the commercial production of goods or specialization of cash crops (UNICEF 1998, 10; UNICEF 2001, 9–10; FAO 2002, 29, 80; Kirk and Sawdon 2002; Smelser 1971, 352).

---

jam factory in Koysinjaq. In Sumail and Suleymaniya the UN made contracts for machines and sent the containers with the equipment, only to learn that there was no building available for the project. The UN then sent a cold-storage car for about US$230,000, but it did not function. The project was passed on to the Italian Meclat Company at 10 percent of the contract, but without success.

23. Khanekah interview.

Tutelage and Toleration

After eleven years of externally generated aid and its semi-legitimizing functions, the Kurdish quasi-state was still nonindustrialized, dependent upon imports for most food and consumption needs, and lacking installation and maintenance of advanced technology. Urbanization processes did not lead to modernization trends across Kurdish society. Refugees that had been resettled to their original villages during the first relief phase either had returned to city centers, fled the country, or become part of poor, urban squatter populations. About 60 percent of the population lived below the poverty line, gaining an average monthly income per person of about US$5, or about US$390 annually for a family of seven. Twenty percent lived in extreme poverty, earning less than US$200 annually per family (FAO 2002, 20–21). In rural areas the annual average income of individual family members was US$115 or about US$10 monthly. About 97 percent of rural populations depended upon WFP-allocated food baskets to sustain daily lives (FAO 2002, 21). Poverty and illiteracy, alongside growing pockets of wealth, gave rise to new social problems: street children, divorce, and single-woman–headed households, including young children quitting school to assist families in income-generating activities.

Economically underdeveloped, institutionally weak, and dependent upon the UN and INGOs for revenues, the Kurdish quasi-state had limited internal sovereignty and leverage in Iraq. The UN took the place of the Iraqi central government without fortifying the ministries and directorates in the Kurdistan Region. It introduced professional procedures and trained Kurdish officials to implement orders; however, the highly centralized programming excluded the KRG from decision making or implementation processes. The UN and Baghdad, and not the KRG, controlled the procurement and distribution of revenues, food supplies, and materials. When OFFP representatives for the Kurdistan Region had meetings with the central government, no Kurdish officials or experts were involved.

Rather, the MOU signed between the UN and the central government in 1996 gave the UN's special agency, the United Nations Office of the Humanitarian Coordinator in Iraq (UNOHCI), the role of acting in behalf of the central government to procure, transport, and distribute humanitarian aid for INGOs and UN agencies to the Kurdistan Region (Volcker, Goldstone, and Pieth 2005, 111–22). Despite the presence of the KRG, the UN acted like the government in the northern region with its specialized agencies operating as ministries: UNOHCI as a council of ministers, HABITAT as a ministry of housing of reconstruction, and UNICEF as a ministry of water and sanitation. In essence, there were two UN programs in Iraq. One was run out of Baghdad, whereby the UN was the trustee for the monies for the sale of oil and purchase of goods and the Iraqi government was the key decision maker. The other program was in the Kurdistan Region and administered by the UN. In this context, the relationship between the Kurdistan Region and the central government was essentially one of tutelage, with all reporting and decision making done in Baghdad.

Indeed, as in the prewar and first relief periods, important linkages continued between the Kurdistan Region and the rest of Iraq based on resource sharing, commercial interests, and social ties. The UNDP's eventual repair of the electricity networks and power substations added a hydroelectric component and generators to the dams in the Kurdistan Region and their reconnection to the national grid. Commercial linkages between the Kurdistan Region and governorates below the green line via Dohuk were also active, despite the closure of key transportation routes. Merchants in Dohuk and their political party patrons benefited from the shifts in trade routes and their geographical proximity to Mosul and the Turkish border. With about 85 percent of OFFP goods transported to the Kurdistan Region via Turkey, they often made political compromises to keep the borders open at Zakho, which became a key smuggling hub. Kurdish contractors and vendors also were required to coordinate with central government agencies before shipping their goods to Mosul and through border points.[24] The central government and/or border guards, in turn, tolerated commercial relations by sporadically opening the internal checkpoints to Kurdish and Arab businessmen. Border openings allowed cultural, religious, and linguistic ties to continue between Kurds and Arabs, including with Christian communities in the Kurdistan Region and Arab Iraq and with Arab-speaking Muslim families.

Yet, as in the prewar and early relief periods, economic and commercial linkages between the Kurdish quasi-state and Baghdad were generally on a personal scale or within a privileged community of private businessmen and political

---

24. For example, if food items were being transported to Dohuk, they first had to go to Zakho, then to Mosul and then to Dohuk, or via Kirkuk.

elites, and not part of legitimate government institutions, official representations, or legal mechanisms of exchange. Local populations were too removed from the benefits from the OFFP to have experienced a sense of improvement in their daily lives as part of the Iraqi state. Most had no access to the electricity flows or the revenues generated from oil-for-food smuggling business. Communications and transportation systems between regions remained blocked by the internal embargo and political party tensions. Cell phones entered the local market in 2000; however, populations could not call Baghdad or outlying areas except via a costly satellite phone. Local populations also had insufficient resources to travel or interact with non-Kurdish communities and remained confined to their localities, particularly as the economic conditions declined in the regions south of the green line.

The relationship between the Kurdish quasi-state and the central government also remained strained because of ongoing authoritarianism and absence of political trust. Instead of attempting to draw Kurds into the central state, Iraqi policies reinforced the distinct sense of Kurdish nationalism that had evolved since the state formation period and the idea of a Kurdish quasi-state apart from Baghdad. Despite occasional border openings, Baghdad maintained the internal embargo and obstructed the OFFP by engaging in indiscriminate violence against relief trucks and workers in the Kurdistan Region. In addition, the central government continued to ethnicize the boundaries and identities of Kirkuk, which reinforced the Kurds' ethnicized claims to the city and heightened political tensions. By 2000, only 1.2 percent of workers in the Northern Petroleum Company in Kirkuk, or about 120 of 10,000, were Kurds (MERA 2007).

Iraqi Kurds were further sensitized to their distinct political conditions and victim status by cross-border Kurdish communities. The ongoing environment of fear and continued repression of Kurds from Turkey, Iran, and Syria mobilized Kurds in the diaspora and the region to use the autonomous Kurdistan Region as a basis for their own political activities. Kurdish nationalist groupings such as the PKK, the Kurdistan Democratic Party of Iran (KDPI), and Komala remained active in the region and were supported in part by the different Iraqi Kurdish groups. Over time, local populations that once ostracized the PKK had come to support it as the only authentic Kurdish nationalist organization struggling for the Kurdish cause. Nor did international actors make any effort to encourage reconciliation, integrate the Kurdistan Region into the Iraqi state, or create

TABLE 3. WORKERS IN THE NORTHERN PETROLEUM COMPANY
IN KIRKUK, 1958–2003.

Year	Arabs	Kurds	Turcomans	Christians	English	Total
1958	40	850	370	900	70	2230
1960	55	1350	500	1100	65	3070
1963	100	1150	700	1400	60	3410
1965	170	1000	800	1350	55	3375
1968	300	875	850	1000	50	3075
1972	900	700	900	1000		3500
1978	2700	500	1200	850		5250
1982	4500	400	1500	800		7200
1988	5200	300	1700	750		7950
1995	6600	260	1800	700		9360
2000	7200	119	1920	600		9839
2003	7300	610	2100	500		10510

Source: MERA 2007.

mechanisms in which Kurdish demands could have been systematically channeled to the central government. As in the first relief period, international politics and the strategic interests of foreign governments warranted against political
negotiations with the rogue Iraqi state. Continuous tensions with Baghdad over
WMD inspections in the country and the ongoing sanctions regime discouraged
any possibility of official linkages with Arbil.

To be sure, during this period the U.S. government provided revenues and
support to Iraqi opposition groups, the majority of which were allocated to
the INC, or about US$78 million in 1998–2002 (Katzman 2005, 45). The Bush
administration sponsored meetings with Iraqi Arab groups and Kurdish leaders in London and foreign capitals to negotiate strategies for creating a federal
system in a post-Saddam Iraq, of which the Kurds were an integral part. Still,
by early 2003 any possible debate over Kurdish autonomy and the territorial
boundaries of the Kurdistan Region was seconded to issues about more stringent
UN resolutions (UNSCR 1441 and 1409), locating WMD in Iraq, engaging in
the post–September 11 "war on terror," and preparing for regime change in Iraq.
These efforts included establishing the operational mechanisms for the Northern

Front, of which the Iraqi Kurds were an integral part, and not building a cohesive Iraqi state or developing a sense of shared Iraqi identity among Iraqi and Kurdish populations.

Conclusions

The OFFP period provided continuity in external aid to the Kurdistan Region that allowed economic recovery and some forms of rehabilitation. It moved beyond the first relief phase by engaging in conflict resolution and offering more expansive aid programs. Ongoing external support provided the semi-legitimacy and internal sovereignty necessary to keep the Kurdish quasi-state alive. Yet the conditionalities of the aid program, tied to the one-Iraq policy, continued to limit the self-sufficiency and leverage of the Kurdish quasi-state. Low levels of internal sovereignty enhanced by domestic cultural constraints, in turn, checked effective internal governance and hindered reform. In the absence of any real change in the regional political economy, and without any access to legal international trade and its integrative structures, the Kurdish quasi-state remained isolated, antagonistic, and without interest or reason to negotiate with Baghdad.

4

The Democracy Mission

WITH THE ANGLO-AMERICAN INTERVENTION in Iraq and overthrow of Saddam Hussein in April 2003, the nature of external aid to the Kurdish quasi-state changed in important ways. Foreign assistance no longer centered on the traditional delivery of goods and services but on capacity building and long-term development. It also recognized the KRG as a legitimate political entity in a federal Iraq, with rights and revenues provided in a new Iraqi constitution. This shift was integrally tied to international politics and U.S. interests in post-Saddam Iraq, which focused on controlling Iraqi petroleum markets, winning the "war on terror," reconstructing the country, and establishing a western-friendly regime based on liberal democratic norms (Carapico 2002, 379). Greater external patronage and international support, alongside patterns of disintegration in the rest of the country, strengthened the Kurdish quasi-state's internal sovereignty and political leverage in the country. The Kurds became power-brokers in Baghdad, as well as commercial negotiators with regional states and foreign governments. Development processes also had unintended consequences on the Kurdistan Region; a more complex political economy encouraged cleavages within Kurdish society and new forms of mobilization and opposition.

Reconstructing One Iraq

As in the first two relief periods, humanitarian assistance played a key role in supporting immediate postwar recovery and rehabilitation in the Kurdistan Region. After 2003, INGOs and foreign governments provided vital relief aid to vulnerable populations, including the swelling refugee and IDP communities. They rebuilt more schools, constructed additional clinics, and supplied necessary food items to local populations. External aid programs reinforced existing civil-society–building efforts, such as training workshops for youth, human rights campaigns, and technical assistance based on anticorruption, violence against women, and civic education.

Yet the particular nature of the third phase of external aid created distinct opportunities and development outcomes for the Kurdistan Region that were unavailable in the earlier phases. For one, the size and scope of the aid program increased exponentially, with the U.S. government assuming the largest proportion of the reconstruction responsibilities and expenses. After the overthrow of Saddam Hussein and the Ba'athist regime, the U.S. government became an occupying force in Iraq, and the Coalition Provisional Authority (CPA) (April 2003–June 2004), headed by L. Paul Bremer III, assumed responsibility for implementing U.S. policies and programs (Katzman 2005, 17).[1] The American government financed Iraqi reconstruction with an initial allocation by the U.S. Congress of about US$18.6 billion. Additional pools of revenues became available: U.S. Congressional supplemental allocations, CPA funds, the Commanders Emergency Response Program (CERP), and the Commander's Humanitarian Relief and Reconstruction Projects (CHHRP) (UNICEF 2004, 66–67; UNSAI 2004, 16; Tarnoff 2004, 2–8, 18; Katzman 2005, 17, 30–43; Sharp and Blanchard 2005, 1).[2] U.S. agencies—the Department of Defense, the State Department, the Department of the Treasury, and the USAID—had their own budgets, administrative procedures, and conditionalities, adding to the size of revenues and the complexity of U.S. funding processes.

The U.S. government's financial stake in post-Saddam Iraq was driven by its strategic interests in reviving and securing access to petroleum and gas resources in the Persian Gulf and Caspian Seas, controlling expenditures of Iraqi oil, managing lucrative reconstruction contracts, and liberalizing the Iraqi economy as a

---

1. In April 2003 Lt. General Jay Garner (ret.) was appointed head of the Department of Defense's Office of Reconstruction and Humanitarian Assistance to direct reconstruction and advise Iraqi ministries. He was replaced by L. Paul Bremer III one month later.

2. Interview with Harry Shute, former commander of the 404th Civil Affairs Battalion, U.S. Army and current advisor to the KRG, Arbil, June 12, 2007. The CERP and CHHRP were DOD funds and considered as "walking-around money" for small reconstruction projects at the village level. In 2004 the total CERP funds in Iraq were about US$549 million, and CHHRP funds were about US$86 million. The latter included some allocations in the Kurdistan Region.

means of promoting free enterprise and development. Underlying these objectives was the Bush administration's belief that a U.S.-allied Iraqi regime could serve as an alternative to Saudi Arabia as a strategic supplier of petroleum and undermine Arab regimes and Iran (Looney 2003a, 576–77; Alkadiri and Mohamedi 2003, 21). The post-Saddam aid program also had a normative component. It was devised around values and efforts of the American government to democratize Iraq in the context of the ongoing U.S. "war on terror" (Schlumberger 2006). This effort meant promoting new norms such as good governance, decentralization, civil-society building, and minority group rights throughout Iraq.

Indeed, the aid program had wide international support. The UN assumed a liaison role in transitioning OFFP operations to postwar recovery programs through the United Nations Assistance Mission for Iraq (UNAMI). The international community contributed financially as well, pledging over US$13 billion at the Madrid Conference in 2004 (Sharp and Blanchard 2005, 1). By January 2005, foreign contributions to reconstruction and stabilization in postwar Iraq were channeled through the Development Fund for Iraq (DFI) and the International Reconstruction Fund Facility for Iraq (IRFFI) and included about US$21 billion in grants, loans, and credits and $30 billion in the theater and inside Iraq (Tarnoff 2005, 21–23). Foreign governments offered necessary security and political assistance as well. The British government co-implemented the intervention and occupation of Iraq and stationed its troops in Basra, alongside U.S. forces in Baghdad and surrounding regions and smaller contingents of South Korean forces (3,500) in the Kurdistan Region. The international military presence continued after the termination of the safe haven and no-fly zones. By 2005 twenty-eight countries had become part of the Multinational Force efforts that included security assistance and training Iraqi troops and police forces. NATO participated in training missions in Iraq alongside noncoalition countries (Sharp and Blanchard 2005, 1–2).

Yet the multilateral character of foreign aid gradually weakened over time with deteriorating security conditions, particularly after the bombing of the UN's Baghdad headquarters in August 2003 and transfer of its operations to Jordan. INGOs and other representations followed, leaving the American government with the largest influence in the Iraqi reconstruction effort. Even after the CPA departed and the Iraqi Governing Council (IGC) was replaced by an elected Iraqi parliament in December 2005, the U.S. government retained ultimate decision-making authority for humanitarian aid and reconstruction projects, as well as running the central government via the American Embassy in Baghdad (Tarnoff 2004, 8–9; Katzman 2005, 30).

Reconstructing Iraq based on democracy mission objectives required a major U.S. policy shift that encouraged external investment and trade by moving the country from recovery to sustainable growth (Looney 2003a; Alkadiri and Mohamedi 2003, 21–22). Whereas prior efforts focused on food and fuel distributions inside the Kurdistan Region, after 2003 the main concern was to stabilize, economically liberalize, and democratize the entire country. This shift involved privatizing Iraqi industries, modernizing the Baghdad stock exchange, reforming the central bank, creating a new currency, offering credit to Iraqi businesses, encouraging private entrepreneurship, rewriting the tax system, and lowering customs tariffs at border areas to facilitate open trade agreements (Looney 2003b). U.S. objectives were further supported by terminating UN sanctions, lifting the internal embargo against the Kurdistan Region, demilitarizing the green line, and removing Iraq from the U.S. list of terrorist states.

In contrast to the first two aid programs, resource allocations skewed revenues away from the Kurdish north toward southern and central Iraq. Rather than invest in the one region of Iraq that was functioning and relatively stable, the U.S. government and foreign donors targeted reconstruction funds to the most unstable parts of the country. The overall sentiment was that the Kurdistan Region was developed enough and that resources needed to be channeled to more insecure regions as a means of depriving the insurgency and winning the "hearts and minds" of Iraqis. This effort focused on quick-impact projects, such as reconnecting the electricity, rebuilding the infrastructure, resettling displaced populations, providing adequate health and education services, and protecting vulnerable populations from insurgent groups.

Whereas the Kurdistan Region received the largest percentage of external assistance during the relief and OFFP programs, after 2003 its allocations declined in relation to the rest of Iraq. Of the US$18.6 billion (excluding supplementals) earmarked for Iraqi reconstruction, less than 4 percent, or about US$1 billion was allocated to the Kurdistan Region (USGAKR 2006).[3] Projects and personnel also

---

3. Of this amount US$143 million was spent or planned to be spent for Suleymaniya, $395 million for Arbil, and $108 million for Dohuk governorates. Additional funds were set aside for the Kurdistan Region, such as economic support funds, flood relief reconstruction projects, etc.

shifted southward. While INGOs refused to sign the MOU and work with the Iraqi government during the first two aid periods, after the downfall of Saddam Hussein they turned to the central and southern regions, where the need for aid seemed to be the greatest. By May 2003 most INGOs were stationed in Baghdad, while only six individuals were responsible for the seven northern governorates, the majority of which were secondarily military experts.

Funding processes were equally skewed. Unlike in earlier programs, aid revenues were channeled to private companies or organizations acting as contractors for the U.S. government and not to small community projects. These organizations included Iraqi security forces, consultancies to Baghdad government ministries, and private security companies hired to protect U.S. business and governmental personnel in Iraq. Many had little interest in coordinating activities with local NGOs or the KRG, but instead reported back to their parent organization at the headquarters office. They also had no previous experience in Iraq, operated independently from the existing system, and remained isolated from local authorities (Tarnoff 2004, 5, 20; Barnett, Eggleston, and Webber 2003, 31).[4] Growing instability in southern and central Iraq, relative security in the Kurdish north, and increasing Kurdish nationalist ambitions further impeded the effective disbursement of program revenues to the Kurdistan Region. By December 2004, only US$2.1 billion of the US$18.6 billion allocated to Iraqi reconstruction by the U.S. Congress had been spent. The following year, only US$1 billion of the US$13 billion pledged to the IRFFI had been disbursed, and 98 percent, or over US$2 million of UN programs, remained unfunded (UNSAI

---

4. Interviews with various INGOs, Arbil, Dec. 2003. A common INGO complaint was the difficulty of accessing donor funds because of complex funding procedures. In contrast to the first relief period, CPA officials did not interact regularly with INGOs but remained "cloistered" in hotels and available by appointment only. Some monthly meetings were organized; however, most INGOs and local organizations had little idea as to who was in charge and what types of revenues were available. Donors also failed to coordinate with existing INGO projects. For example, the INGO Qandil built thirteen houses in Makhmur village, which is under the official administrative jurisdiction of Baghdad but part of a UNHCR project and de facto controlled by the KRG. Qandil had a blueprint for each house and a standard number of materials, including spindar that it distributed to each family. A U.S. delegation came to visit and promised the villages concrete roofing, without knowing that the families already had received the spindar, which was then sold in the local market.

2004, 12–13; Tarnoff 2004). Overtime budgets for water, sewerage, and electricity decreased while security and democratization assumed increasing priority.

Aid revenues also were increasingly used as a means of depriving the insurgency. When the USAID arrived in Iraq in June 2004, it took US$500 million of the $600 million targeted to the Kurdistan Region and reallocated it to other regions in Iraq, particularly in Sunni Arab regions (Katzman 2005, 30). The concern was to prevent the Kurdistan north from advancing too far in relation to the rest of the country and to concentrate U.S. funds on troubled regions.[5] By late 2004, of the total U.S. government spending in Iraq, 32 percent was allocated to security, 16 percent to democratization, and 51 percent to infrastructure development (Tarnoff 2004, 14).

The Benefits of Stalemate

Given the apparent financial disadvantages of the aid program, what explains the transformations in the Kurdistan Region since 2003? Instead of becoming mired in insecurity and chaos like the southern and central regions—recipients of the majority of aid resources—the Kurdish north remained relatively stable, which permitted some sectors of the economy to recover and thrive. Political openings also emerged over time, creating a more expansive arena for different civil-society groups to mobilize.

Despite the focus on the central and southern regions, the democracy mission offered new forms of external patronage and international support to the Kurdish quasi-state, which enhanced its legitimacy and leverage in a federal Iraq. The U.S. emphasis on regional and ethnic group quotas as a means of determining the distribution of resources, the Transitional Law for the Administration of Iraq signed in March 2004 (TAL), and the 2005 Iraqi constitution provided the KRG with recognition, rights, and revenues as a distinct political entity. Article 117 specifically recognized the Kurdistan Region as an integral component of a federal Iraq with both Kurdish and Arabic as the official languages (Barkey 2009, 11–12). The devolution of power to the regions also expanded the KRG's internal sovereignty within its official territorial boundaries. Decentralization, rooted in

5. Shute interview.

article 56 of the TAL, established mechanisms for power-sharing between the central and regional governments, including the creation of provincial councils as legitimate centers in which political decisions, resource allocations and administrative appointments could be made.

In contrast to previous periods, when the KRG was alienated from the central government, after 2003 it gained important representation in Baghdad. Leading Kurdish officials were appointed to high-level positions: Hoshyr Zibari as foreign minister, Nasreen Barwari as minister of public works, Barham Salih as minister of planning and vice prime minister, and Jelal Talabani as president. Kurds also accessed high administrative posts in disputed territories. Immediately after the overthrow of Saddam Hussein, the CPA appointed a Kurd as mayor of Tel Afar, despite the Kurds' clear minority status in the province (Olson 2005, 123). In Ninevah and Kirkuk the Kurds received key administrative and political positions, often outnumbering Arab majority populations.

Federalist structures gave the KRG the authority to alter Iraqi laws not relating to foreign policy, national security, or financial issues; to control its own police and security forces; and to manage natural resources in the region, including rights to exploit and administer certain petroleum fields (Katzman 2005, 5). Official mechanisms also became available to address unresolved boundary issues. In contrast to previous periods, whereby the Kirkuk issue was part of back-door discussions conducted between Iraqi presidents and Kurdish leaders during sporadic ceasefires, it became part of constitutional processes within a decentralized political system. Article 58 of the TAL, replaced by article 140 of the Iraqi constitution, situates Kirkuk within the larger problem of negotiating all of Iraq's disputed territories. This effort includes (1) resettling Arabs to their original lands; (2) resettling expelled Kurds back to Kirkuk; (3) reshaping administrative units in Kirkuk to their pre-1976 status; and (4) conducting a census and referendum to decide whether the province will be administered by the central government or the KRG.

New economic development opportunities also became available for the Kurdish quasi-state. Whereas conditionalities of the previous aid programs prohibited INGOs, UN agencies, and foreign governments from working directly with the KRG, the democracy mission permitted direct funding and support to the Kurdistan Region as part of a federal Iraq (Natali 2005). Although the Kurdish north received a small share of the Iraqi reconstruction budget, total revenues allocated to the region increased exponentially. In contrast to the US$4.1–6.1 billion received during the six-year OFFP, by December 2003 the democracy mission, through the DFI, allocated US$4 billion to the two Kurdish administrations, which included the unspent OFFP funds paid to the Kurds outside regular financing to complete unfinished UN projects (Olson 2005, 170). From March to November 2003, the KRG-Suleymaniya's annual budget rose from US$200 million to over $1 billion.[6]

In particular, the 2005 Iraqi constitution granted the Kurdistan Region an annual capital investment budget of 17 percent of the federal budget, which after deductions increased from US$2.5 billion to over $6 billion annually in 2005–9 (*Hawlati* 2007b).[7] To further encourage decentralization at the regional level, Baghdad allocated revenues to the Kurdistan Region's provincial councils through the special Advanced Development Provincial Reconstruction (ADPR) budget.[8] From 2006 to 2008 the ADPR budget for the three Kurdish governorates increased from US$130 million to $395 million. Each Kurdish province also received a security budget. In 2003–4 the CPA allocated Arbil governorate US$440 million for its security needs.[9]

Moreover, the Kurdistan Region accessed a more comprehensive aid regime. In contrast to previous programs, external assistance moved beyond short-term relief to capacity and infrastructure building at the national and local levels. Of

6. Interviews with Abdul-Razzaq Mirza, former director of the Investment Promotion Board of Suleymaniya, Suleymaniya, Dec. 12, 2005; Khaffaf interview.

7. Ahmad interview. The deductions include food allocations, the presidency of Baghdad, and pilgrimages, and leave the actual allocation at about 13 percent. There is also contention over the total amount actually provided for the Kurdistan Region, which is based on a fluctuating price of oil sales.

8. Interviews with Mustafa Ahmed Abdullhalig, director of development and modification center, Dohuk Governorate, Dohuk, Jan. 3, 2008; Salih interview. The ADPR has helped advance decentralized efforts by strengthening the size and scope of regional directorates and providing alternative revenues for diverse offices within the governorates, including the governor, mayor, submayor, and villages. Budgets for the Kurdistan Region do not include allocations for the disputed territories. The provincial councils have channeled revenues from alternative budgets to these regions. For instance, Dohuk governorate pays for Singar and Sheikhan regions even though they are not included in the Dohuk provincial council budget. The Baghdad government provides Mosul with about US$400 million and Sheikhan with $2 million.

9. Shute interview.

TABLE 4. PROVINCIAL COUNCIL BUDGETS FOR THE KURDISTAN
REGION, 2006–2008 (IN MILLION USD).

	2006	2007	2008
Dohuk[a, b]	30	72	91
Arbil	48	115	145
Suleymaniya	52	127	159
Total	130	314	395

Source: Ministry of Finance, Iraqi Central Government, U.S. Treasury, OPA Reports, and documents from provincial councils of Suleymaniya, Dohuk, and Arbil.
[a]The allocation for the Dohuk council increased about 20 percent from 2006 to 2007 because Baghdad initially excluded
Akre, claiming it was part of Mosul administration. The allocation for Akre was included thereafter.
[b]Of the total provincial budget in Dohuk, 80 percent is allocated to trade, 14 percent to construction, and 6 percent to industry and factories.

the Iraqi reconstruction budget provided to the Kurdistan Region, US$602 million, or about 93 percent, was allocated to construction, including infrastructure building such as water-treatment plants and power transmission substations (USGAKR 2006). These revenues helped create an industrial zone, hydropower stations, road rehabilitation, private-sector development, and microwave links connecting cities such as Suleymaniya, Arbil, and Kirkuk to the rest of Iraq, including Baghdad, Baquba, Basra, and um Qasr. In coordination with the KRG Ministry of Planning, the U.S. military assisted international companies and NGOs to invest in the region and helped oversee the construction of a US$10.2 million electricity network, including transmission lines and fiber-optic cables to transfer data and improve communication across Iraq (USAID/IRAQ 2008, 34). It also established the Civil Police Transition Teams (CPTT) that provided materials, equipment, and skills to Iraq and the Kurdistan Region. From 2003 to 2005 the CPTT trained and armed over 4,000 Kurdish security forces in warfare tactics in the same types of schools in which U.S. special forces are trained.[10]

Foreign governments and international institutions offered additional assistance. From 2003 to 2007 the South Korean government spent US$260 million

10. Interview with anonymous military and security source, Arbil, Jan. 13, 2007.

for humanitarian relief activities in Iraq, 47 percent (US$120,000) of which was allocated to the Kurdistan Region. These contributions included high technology, expertise, and vehicles for the regional government.[11] Capacity-building projects increased over time, particularly after the departure of the CPA and the acceptance of regional federalism for the KRG by foreign governments and international organizations. National capacity-building projects supported by the USAID Regional Reconstruction Team (RRT) and the World Bank focused on local governance, policy reform, service delivery, public participation, civil society, decision making, and infrastructure building in the Kurdish north.[12]

Internal Sovereignty and Development

With larger revenues and greater internal sovereignty, the Kurdish-quasi state assumed a greater role in advancing political and economic development. Using the 2005 Iraqi constitution as a template and with a special parliamentary committee in place, the Kurdish elites redrafted a regional constitution that incorporated general principles of civic, cultural, and political rights and religious freedom into the region's governance structure. Political processes and institutions also became more representative to include diverse parties and ethnic and religious groups. Despite their ongoing political differences, the KDP and PUK decided to run on one unified Kurdistani List for the Iraqi parliament and a Kurdistan National Democratic List for the KNA for the December 2005 legislative elections in Baghdad and Arbil respectively. The parties also suppressed the 7 percent threshold to encourage small party participation in the elections.[13]

11. Interviews with Mr. Kim Sikhyon, assistant resident representative, Korea International Cooperation Agency (KOICA) Office in Iraq (Arbil), and Mr. Jun Byung-Wook, first secretary, Arbil Liaison Office, Embassy of the Republic of Korea, Zaytun Division, Arbil, Mar. 12, 2008.

12. Interviews with Mehmet Pel, manager of Protect Project, Arbil, Jan. 25, 2008, and Abdalla G. Mohammed, regional program director, northern region, local governance program-Iraq, Research Triangle Institute (RTI), Arbil, Dec. 19, 2006. The World Bank–funded road construction project in Altun Kopri implemented by Protect Project is valued at US$35 million.

13. Interview with Ms. Khaman Zrar Asaad, member of the IKP, Arbil, Apr. 12, 2007. The 2005 parliamentary electoral campaign involved two lists, one for the central government representatives

Kurdish officials created a semi-unified and more expansive government. In their attempt to address the "serious issues ahead" and to mobilize local populations in the Kurdistan Region, on January 21, 2006, Ma'soud Barzani and Jelal Talabani signed the Unification Agreement, which established the framework in which the two parties could co-govern the region once again (KRG 2006). To this end, in May 2006 the KDP and PUK merged their administrations into one regional government and established the institutional mechanisms that allowed them to share and separate power among themselves, much the way they tried to do in 1992 under the "50-50 split." KRG party officials divided key ministries between the KDP and PUK and appointed new ministers, many of whom did not even have ministries (*wazir bey wazirat*), to the government. The objective was to "keep the peace" between the parties, who still distrusted each other, and to stabilize the region for investment purposes.

Whereas the first KNA had comprised the two main political parties (KDP and PUK) and the ADM, the composition of the fifth National Assembly established in May 2006 included 111 seats representing fourteen political parties and one independent individual.[14] Small parties also were incorporated into the newly created High Committee of Consultants and specialized parliamentary committees, which allowed them to examine important issues such as the Kurdistan constitution, electricity needs, unification processes, and implementing article 140 of the Iraqi constitution. Women gained political participation as well, representing nearly 30 percent of the total members of the KNA. By 2009 the renamed Iraqi Kurdistan Parliament (IKP) had lowered the age for membership from thirty to twenty-five years, creating greater spaces for the young generation to participate in political life.

---

and one for the KNA. The Islamic Society of Kurdistan refused to participate in the Kurdistani List and ran independently.

14. Nuri Talabani interview. The total seats that the Kurds won in the 275 seat Baghdad parliament was 58, down from 75 in the January 2005 elections. The Kurdistan Alliance won 53 seats and the Islamic Union list won 5 seats. For the KNA, the Kurdistan National Democratic List won 104 seats, with the distribution of seats as follows: KDP, 40 (including deputy of parliament speaker and secretary of the parliament; PUK, 39 (including Dr. Nuri Talabani and parliament speaker); Kurdistan Communist Party, 2; Islamic Union of Kurdistan, 9; Turcoman, 4; Kurdistan National Democratic Union, 1; Assyrians, 5; and the Kurdistan Toilers party, 1.

With its vast resources from the central government, the KRG also assumed a leading role in promoting economic development. After 2003 the Kurdistan Region started behaving like a quasi-developmental state, intervening in economic life with the specific purpose of promoting foreign direct investment. Instead of completely reviving the Iraqi social-welfare state, creating a free market with a minimal state role that ensures the widest range of individual freedoms, or lobbying for NGO assistance, the KRG has attempted to construct a partnership with major economic interests, underpinned by Kurdish nationalist priorities. A key component of this development strategy focuses on private-sector growth. In a speech to an International Trade Show in Suleymaniya, former prime minister Netchervan Barzani (2006–9) emphasized his support for private-sector development, assuring potential investors that "Kurdistan is open for business" ("Kurdistan PM's Speech" 2006). Since 2003 the KRG has sent delegations of economists to South Korea for training and to discuss strategies for growth and development based on the Southeast Asian experience. It later declared Dubai a development model for the region.

In the attempt to move away from a state-controlled economy to a market-oriented one, the KRG has sold or rented out state-owned industries to individuals or foreign companies, decreased taxes on construction projects while assuming most project costs, sponsored annual trade fairs in the region, and assumed a greater role in managing the commercial sector. In 2006 the KRG passed one of the most liberal investment laws of its kind in the Middle East.[15] It also applied its perceived constitutional rights to exploit petroleum resources in the Kurdistan Region. In August 2007 the KRG passed a hydrocarbons law for the region and started discussions with international companies to construct a network of pipelines planned to be linked to the Iraqi strategic pipeline in Kirkuk.

15. Tutinçi interview; interview with Ferda Cilalioglu Cemiloglu, director, Tigris Company, Shorush and Arbil, Dec. 1, 2005. The Iraqi investment law requires foreign businesses to establish joint ventures with an Iraqi-owned company, providing for a 51–49 percentage agreement (51 percent for Iraqi firms). Key components of the Kurdistan Region investment law are: (1) businesses are free to bring in money with no taxes on their investment profit; (2) land rental at minimal payments; (3) free transfer of money abroad with the right to sell at any time; and (4) international guarantees for protection of investments.

TABLE 5. FACTORIES IN ARBIL THAT RECEIVED LICENSES FROM
THE KRG GENERAL DIRECTORATE OF INDUSTRY, 1995–2006.

Types of factories	No. of factories	No. of workers	Investment in ID	% of total factories
Building & construction	383	1,187	18,997,000,000	34.160
Metal	229	307	7,150,500,000	20.428
Food (agro-industry)	167	308	11,187,000,000	14.897
Plastic	77	166	1,198,000,000	6.864
Service	75	558	1,980,000,000	6.690
Wood making	59	211	820,000,000	5.263
Chemical	31	476	4,365,000,000	2.765
Aluminum	26	54	259,500,000	2.319
Woven textiles	13	100	231,885,000	1.159
Other	58	309	2,317,000,000	5.441

Source: Kurdistan Regional Government, Ministry of Industry, General Directorate of Industry, Arbil, 2007.

Kurdish quasi-state-led investment has jump-started the local economy. From 2001 to 2009 the KRG helped create 1,376 private industrial projects, employing over 14,184 workers at a value of over 500 billion ID (KRG-MOI, 2007). During this same period the private sector in Suleymaniya governorate received over US$1 billion worth of contracts, while the KRG in Arbil provided an additional US$35 million to contractors. From 2006 to December 2008 the KRG approved more than US$4 billion worth of private development projects, mainly in construction, tourism, and petroleum industries (USAID/IRAQ 2008, 29). The KRG general directorate of industry awarded 1,121 private factories in Arbil licenses, 34 percent of which were based in building and construction and 20 percent in metal factories.[16] Similarly, 95 percent of the development in Dohuk governorate has been in the private sector, the most important of which has been in construction and tourism, with new luxury hotels and restaurants

16. Interviews with Taha Ismail Mohammed, member of the council of ministers, KRG, Arbil, Jan. 9, 2007, and Dana Majid, governor of Suleymaniya, Suleymaniya, Dec. 1, 2007; Hawrami interview; Khaffaf interview. Large factories have 100 workers or more, medium-sized ones have 20–100 workers, and small factories have 20 or fewer.

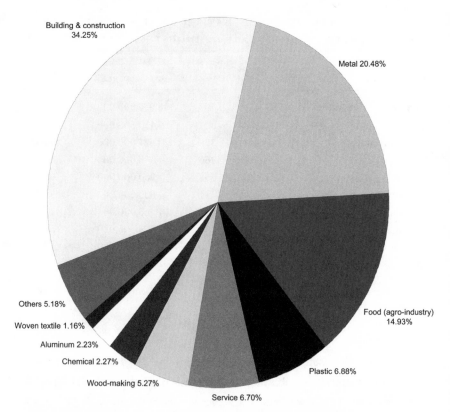

Building & construction
34.25%

Metal 20.48%

Food (agro-industry)
14.93%

Plastic 6.88%

Service 6.70%

Wood-making 5.27%

Chemical 2.27%

Aluminum 2.23%

Woven textile 1.16%

Others 5.18%

10. Percentage of factories in Arbil that received licenses from the KRG General Directorate of Industry, 1995–2006. *Source:* KRG, Ministry of Industry, General Directorate of
Industry, Arbil, 2007.

catering to the growing business and international community. From 1992 to
2007 the number of three-star hotels in Dohuk governorate increased from ten
to seventy-four.[17] By December 2008 construction had become the fastest-grow-
ing sector in the regional economy and was estimated at US$2.8 billion (USAID/
IRAQ 2008, 26).

International companies have responded to KRG investment initiatives by
establishing operations in the region (Sliman 2002, 139). In contrast to previous

17. Interviews with Ayad A. Abdulhalim, May 14, 2007, and Jan. 3, 2008.

periods, whereby foreign businesses were virtually absent from the Kurdish north, after 2003 about 20 percent of the construction sector was controlled by international companies. A significant part of private-sector investment has targeted the petroleum industry, alongside construction. By November 2009 the KRG negotiated over thirty oil production sharing contracts (PSCs) with European, American, and South Korean companies or in cooperation with the Kurdistan Exploration and Production Company (KEPCO), valued at over US$10 billion in investment.[18] These companies include the American petroleum conglomerate Hunt Oil, the Korean National Oil Company (KNOC), and Crescent Petroleum/Dana Gas. An important component of the PSCs include infrastructure and capacity building, including rehabilitating schools, constructing refineries, and providing water supplies and electricity to local populations in the Kurdistan Region (USAID/IRAQ 2008, 46, 54).[19]

With a larger revenue base, the Kurdish quasi-state also expanded its social-welfare function. After 2003 the KRG in Arbil (KDP) increased per capita government expenditures to about US$1,000 per person and placed revenues into cash facilities.[20] It constructed public housing and health-care facilities and assumed responsibility for public health-care provision, including the pharmaceutical- and medical-supply distribution system for the region (USAID/IRAQ 2008, 32). By December 2008 the KRG Ministry of Health (MOH) procured about 70 percent of essential medical items, equipment, and technology through private tenders and funded new hospitals, medical specialists, continuing medical education centers (CME), oxygen factories, and medical equipment and supplies to the disputed areas (ODHD 2007). Moreover, the KRG had become the largest employer in the region, providing monthly employment stipends to an estimated

18. Interview with Hawre Azad Riwandizi, marketing executive, Crescent Petroleum–Dana Gas Joint Venture, Jan. 27, 2009, Arbil. The PSCs are a source of contention between the KRG and Baghdad. They differ significantly from the technical support agreements (TSAs) negotiated between foreign companies and the Iraqi central government because they offer foreign companies larger profit-sharing arrangements and benefits.

19. Mr. Jun Byung-Wook interview. For instance, as part of its PSC the KNOC has promoted "oil for development," which involves using future oil profits to renovate schools and engage in capacity-building projects in the Kurdistan Region.

20. Fattah interview.

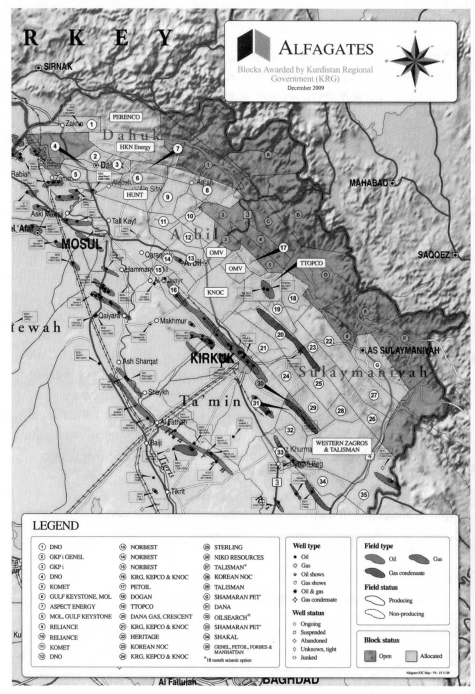

11. Map of oil concessions in the Kurdistan Region. Courtesy of Alphagates, Arbil.

TABLE 6. SCHOOLS, STUDENTS, AND TEACHERS IN THE KURDISTAN
REGION, 2009–2010.

Stages	No. schools	No. students	No. teachers
Kindergarten	241	37,221	2,722
Primary (grades 1–6)	4,468	1,126,781	70,925
Secondary, preparatory (grades 6–12)	694	208,610	12,551
Vocational, institute	131	23,571	2,753
Totals	5,534	1,396,183	88,951

Source: Ministry of Education, KRG, 2010.

1.5 million people in the public sector, or about 76 percent of the population
(ISAID/IRAQ 208, 15).

Educational services expanded to accommodate the pressing demands of the
young generation and the KRG's need to create a skilled and professional workforce. Building upon developments since 1992, the KRG Ministry of Education
(MOE) altered school curricula, translated Arabic textbooks into Kurdish, added
Kurdish culture and history to existing Iraqi history, and constructed hundreds
of new schools and learning facilities across the region (KRG-MOE 2009). By
2010, at the kindergarten, primary, intermediate, and vocational-technical levels,
the Kurdistan Region had 5,534 schools, 1,396,129 students, and 88, 951 teachers (KRG-MOE 2010).[21] Democracy mission norms—human rights, religious
freedom, and gender equality—were incorporated into the academic curricula,
while English was adopted as a second language in all schools (KRG-MOE 2009;
Zaher-Draey 2005, 36).

The Kurdish elites even attempted to engineer social reform. In response to
international criticism and local pressures since 2003, it launched campaigns to
educate and sensitize populations to the ongoing killing of women, particularly
after the filmed, brutal stoning and death of a seventeen-year-old Ezidi woman
named Do'a in April 2007. Alongside existing laws against honor killing, the
KRG established a special parliamentary committee and engaged international

21. The vast majority of this number is primary schools (4,468). Similarly, of the total number
of students 1,126, 781 are at the primary level, with 70,925 teachers.

organizations and academic institutions to investigate honor crimes and other forms of violence against women and children in the Kurdistan Region. In early 2009 Prime Minister Netchervan Barzani met with Kurdish mullahs from the mosques and informed them that they could no longer mention pejorative issues about women in Friday prayers.

From the Bazaar to Semi–Market Exchange

Attempts to create an open market economy have opened new avenues for commerce and trade. The termination of the international sanctions regime and the CPA's cancellation or reduction of customs taxes at all border points in Iraq, without redeveloping the Iraqi system of standardization and classification of goods entering the country, paved the way for cheap imports to flood local markets. Electronic equipment, low-quality goods, expired food products, and inauthentic designer goods have become part of the lucrative trading market encouraged by open borders and the absence of quality control measures in post-Saddam Iraq. As consumer tastes, livelihoods, and demands shifted to imported goods, the role of the Kurdistan Region as a transit zone has revived. Foreign currency and official commercial trade have replaced the subsistence and smuggling economy, while goods and services have become part of an independent exchange system (Sliman 2002, 139; Smelser 1971, 356–58).

To be sure, the informal bazaar-cash economy remains a defining feature of the local economy, just as it was in previous periods. Petroleum continues to flow unofficially across borders, smuggled cigarettes are imported and re-exported to Turkey for large profits, and scrap metal is shipped to Iran from Baghdad via the Kurdish transit zone, all in cash and outside an official banking or insurance system.[22] Still, in contrast to previous periods, external patronage and recognition have allowed the Kurdish quasi-state to access international markets and diversify its economic activities, available goods, and mechanisms for financial exchange. An array of technology, food items, construction materials, and cars from China, Dubai, Saudi Arabia, Kuwait, Jordan, Syria, Turkey, Iran, and southern Iraq

---

22. For instance, one MT of scrap metal in Iraq costs about US$20. After purchasing an export license (which can be difficult to obtain) for US$60, traders can make large profits by selling the metal to Iranian merchants for US$380 per MT.

regularly pass though the Kurdistan transit zone via ports in Mersin, Basra, and Aqaba. China has become particularly popular among the emergent group of international traders who purchase low-quality textile and household items for resale in Iraqi Kurdistan. The owners of Sana Cell in Suleymaniya, for instance, have created a market for ready-made Kurdish clothes produced in China for a fraction of their price in local markets.

Commercial relations have expanded with foreign businesses and regional states. As part of their strategy to assure open borders and develop the region, some Kurdish elites have invited the Turkish government to "invade economically and not militarily."[23] Since 2003 Turkey has established important economic and political interests and pursued a strategy of trade and business in the Kurdistan Region. A protocol established between the Ministries of Petroleum in Iraq and Turkey allows the Baghdad government to send crude oil to Turkey, where it is refined and sent back to Iraq and the Kurdistan Region and sold to local populations at subsidized prices.[24] In 2009 over 250 Turkish companies were operating in Arbil alone, half of which are Kurdish-owned. In Suleymaniya, over half of 500 foreign companies in the governorate are Turkish and Iranian.[25] Big Turkish companies such as Jenkisar, Yedigun, Çevikler, and Nursoy have implemented large-scale development and construction projects, including the new Arbil and Suleymaniya airports, roads, and the proposed industrial city. Turkish companies control 95 percent of the construction market. By late 2007 the value of construction projects implemented by Turkish companies was over US$2.6 billion (USAID/IRAQ 2008, 26). The vast majority of food and consumer items in the Kurdistan Region are imported from Turkey as well.

23. Nowsherwan Mustafa Amin interview.

24. Interview with Mohammed Towfiq, Suleymaniya, Dec. 12, 2005. This arrangement costs the Iraqi central government about US$6 billion annually. Attempts to alter this arrangement, including closure of key transportation routes via Ibrahim Khalil or refusal of Turkish truckers to transport diesel, have directly affected local petroleum/diesel market prices. From June 2005 to November 2007, for instance, the price of gasoline in Iraqi Kurdistan increased from 5,000 to 25,000 ISD per 20 liters, or from US$3.50 to US$20. There are also gangs controlling the local pumping stations in the Kurdistan Region by withholding benzene in an attempt to increase prices and make greater profits.

25. Hawrami interview.

In contrast to the early relief periods, whereby Turkish companies were sent by the Turkish government to Iraqi Kurdistan, after 2003 they arrived as part of an open tendering process, although within the existing government-influenced structure. Some of the most important investment projects are owned by Turkish generals, who in turn, subcontract them to Turkish businesses at a lower price. Most of these companies have arranged special protocols allowing them to bring in their own materials, workers and professional staff, and have marginal engagement with local populations or resources. Still, having been cut off from technical expertise for decades, Iraqi Kurdistan has benefited from Turkish specialization, particularly for finishing on construction projects, trade development, and much-needed services.

By late 2007 the value of Turkish exports to Iraq was about US$2.8–3.5 billion, the majority of which passed through the Kurdistan Region's border points at Ibrahim Khalil (Habur) (USAID/IRAQ 2008, 89). Whereby Zakho was previously a desolate outpost guarded by Iraqi military forces or a hub for regional smuggling, it has become the center of a multi-million-dollar cross-border trade operation with the capacity for receiving 2,000 trucks daily.[26] Commercial opportunities have expanded over time. Large-scale fiber-optics projects implemented by Turkish companies link parts of Zakho to electricity sources from Turkey flowing to Mosul. The Dohuk Chamber of Commerce indicated its preference for Turkish companies to work on petroleum contracts as a means of facilitating future commercial activities and alleviating potential conflict.[27] Turkey's business initiatives also have attracted Kurdish interests across borders. At the annual international trade fair in Diyarbakir in 2005 (Diyarbekir: A Gateway to the Middle East Market), four buses of Iraqi Kurdish businessmen attended alongside high-level Turkish politicians and businessmen, including Kurdish counterparts from Diyarbekir. The Kurdish governor of Diyarbekir opened the conference with a welcome in Kurdish, emphasizing that Kurds and Turks were not just economic friends but also cultural and political ones.[28]

Commercial relations with Iran have strengthened as well, particularly in Suleymaniya governorate, which shares three official and two unofficial border

26. Ahmad interview.
27. Abdulhalim interview, Dohuk, Jan. 3, 2008.
28. Cemiloglu interview.

12. Construction site in Arbil, 2008. Courtesy of Ali Ayverdi.

points, and 450 kilometers of border with its eastern neighbor. To encourage cross-border trade, Kurdish officials established a "free-trade zone" for Iranian products, and they purchase much-needed electricity from Iran. In 2007 cross-border trade with Iran included 100–200 trucks daily that accounted for about 60 percent of the merchants' needs in Suleymaniya province and was valued at US$1 billion (USAID/IRAQ 2008, 89; *Hawlati* 2007a).[29] Of 120 Iranian companies in the Kurdistan Region, about 80 are working in Suleymaniya province and have an important share of the market trade in housing and food materials (*Hawlati* 2007a). Iran has virtual control of plastic, cement, and low-density polyvinyl chloride (PVC) in the Suleymaniya construction market, and its contractors from Iran have constructed the Azman Tunnel in the city.

In the quest to increase its economic leverage, the Kurdish quasi-state has reached out to regional Arab Gulf states, including Egypt, Dubai, Kuwait,

29. Mirza interview; Hawrami interview. The official border points are Bashmaq, Haji Omran, and Perwizkhan.

Lebanon, Jordan, and the United Arab Emirates (UAE). Half of the US$15 billion invested in the Kurdistan Region in 2007–8 was from the Arab Gulf region and focused on large-scale oil and gas production projects (USAID/IRAQ 2008, 90). The Middle East's largest regional private-sector natural gas company, Dana Gas PJSC, has implemented extensive drilling campaigns and has started developing a "Kurdistan Gas City" in the northern region.[30] Egyptian companies have assumed management of former state-run factories, and Lebanese entrepreneurs have established restaurants, private educational institutions, and distributorships. Less significant ties have developed between the KRG and Syria. The reopening of the Syrian-Iraqi trade route from Rahiyya to Mosul and the creation of a free-trade agreement between Syria and Baghdad in 2001 diminished the usage and importance of the small Feshkabor border in Dohuk governorate.

Socioeconomic Differentiation and Political Opposition

The KRG's focus on trade and investment has encouraged shifts in employment and demographic changes. Most important is the move away from agricultural activities to service-sector jobs. To be sure, the KRG and INGOs have attempted to reinvigorate agricultural production, which still represents a source of livelihood in the Kurdistan Region. Donor agencies have targeted millions of dollars to rural development, irrigation, and livestock services.[31] The KRG also has supported outside experts to improve agricultural efficiency, as well as partially subsidizing fuel, fertilizers, and pesticides for farmers. From 2005 to 2006 wheat production actually rose in the Kurdistan Region by 100,000 MT. Vegetable cultivation also increased, providing revenue sources for local farmers and women (ICRC 2007, 22). Still, agricultural production has declined by nearly half since the first aid period, from about 650,000 MT to 338,000 MT (ICRC 2007, 21). Absence of a comprehensive program to encourage agricultural exports and ongoing reliance on the PDS has created a situation in which imported items represent an important proportion of family expenses, instead of locally produced goods.

30. Riwandizi interview.

31. Interview with Jean-Pierre Nereyabagabo, senior agronomist and livelihoods specialist, International Committee of the Red Cross, Arbil, Nov. 11, 2007.

This pattern has been encouraged by demographic trends. Educational and employment opportunities, wage differentials, and lack of services in rural areas have pulled rural communities toward the cities and created additional disincentives to farm (USAID/IRAQ 2008, 16). Most of the young prefer to work in the newly emerged security sector or with private companies, which offer better-paying jobs. Whereas by 2010 an agricultural engineer with a master's degree could earn US$340-550 monthly (400,000–650,000 NID), a security police officer with no advanced diploma could earn US$425–595. By 2004 over 90 percent of the population was urban and 9 percent rural, with only 6 percent working in the agriculture sector (ICRC 2007, 9; ILCS 2005, 1:110).

Urbanization trends and shifting employment structures have helped create a more complex division of labor and changes in the standard of living. The transition from a subsistence economy to one based on semimarket commercial exchange or partial reliances on free market structures has increased the demand for laborers and established patterns of behavior outside the family unit (Smelser 1971, 356). In Arbil more than five hundred Kurds from Turkey are employed as construction workers for the Tigris Company alone. Populations from Suleymaniya and Dohuk also have moved to Arbil to find more lucrative and interesting employment opportunities. Other companies engage workers across borders, opening the labor market to the larger Kurdish and international community. In the tourist town of Shaqlawa, for instance, Iranian Kurds work as wage laborers in the expanding construction market.[32] Daily workers from southern and central Iraq and "guest-workers" from Africa and Asia also have become part of the new market structure, providing cheap labor to government agencies, private contracting companies, and the nouveaux riche (Safa 1982, 8).[33]

The influx of expatriate workers and companies has spurred a construction boom and a form of "casino capitalism" in the main cities (Nijman 2002, 156). Migrations of families from central and southern Iraq to the north, the return of Iraqi Kurdish exiles purchasing or renting their homes as investment property, and the international presence caused rents and prices to skyrocket. In certain

32. Interview with M. Buhari, owner of the Safin Motel, Shaqlawa, Nov. 10, 2005.

33. Akirawy interview; interviews with Beshdar Ahmad, General Directorate of Planning, KRG Ministry of Finance, Arbil, Nov. 13, 2007, and Mohammad Abas Goran, director of finance monitoring, KRG Ministry of Planning, Arbil, Nov. 28, 2007.

TABLE 7. MONTHLY WAGES AND EARNINGS IN THE KURDISTAN
REGION,[a] 2003–2010, IN THOUSAND NID[b] (USD).[c]

	2003-7	2010
Public sector (civil servants)		
Security police	411–700 (334–569)	500–700 (423–593)
Police officer	340–430 (276–350)	700–900 (593–763)
Imam	444–552 (361–449)	500–650 (424–551)
Schoolteacher[d]	264–328 (215–267)	350–600 (297–508)
Doctor	574–713 (467–580)	600–950 (508–805)
Agric. engineer	342–426 (278–346)	400–650 (339–551)
Judge	740–920 (602–748)	800–1,000 (678–847)
Pensioner (*peshmerga*)	60 (49)	150 (127)
Driver	83–104 (67–85)	120–180 (102–153)
Private sector		
Engineer	1,000 (813)	1,220 (1,034)
Senior engineer	2,500 (2,032)	2,750 (2,330)
Taxi driver (daily)[e]	45 (37)	40–65 (34–55)
Shopkeeper[f]	600 (488)	1,000 (847)
Wage laborer (daily)	18–25 (15–20)	30 (25)
Skilled laborer (daily)	—	90 (76)
Mason (daily)	—	70 (59)

Source: Documents from Ministry of Finance and Economy, Directorate General of Finance, Kurdistan Regional Government, April, 2007 and 2009.
Note: High end of range reflects ten years of service with a clean record.
[a]Amounts are based on the starting salary until year ten (last level). An employee not need start at level one or progress annually through each level. One can advance horizontally because of character, contacts, or merit. Police and security officers are waiting to have salaries increased to levels paid in Baghdad.
[b]Average exchange rate during this period was 1.230 NID:US$1.
[c]Exchange rate is 1.180 NID:US$1.
[d]Excludes year-end bonus.
[e]This amount varies depending upon work conditions.
[f]One single-room shop, open daily.

quarters such as Ainkawa or in north Arbil, foreign firms pay between US$2,000 to $4,000 monthly for an average house rental.[34] The rapid increase in demand for construction activities, limited capacity of the three Kurdish cement factories, and dependence upon imported goods also has affected purchase prices (USAID/IRAQ 2008, 28).[35] From 1996 to 2010, land prices for a 250-square-meter plot in Arbil city increased from about US$5,000 to $153,000, while housing costs rose to $423 per meter (see table 7).

Employment, economic, and demographic trends have increased standards of living and encouraged lifestyle changes. Whereas the OFFP generated revenues for a small but privileged group of independent entrepreneurs, the opportunities created by the aid program have influenced average Kurdish families. In December 2004, the median per capita household income in the Kurdistan Region was 21,180 NID, the highest among all the regions in Iraq and above the national average of 17,230 NID (ILCS 2005: 1:141). By 2009, the Kurdistan regional economy had grown from 8 to 25 percent per year over the past several years (USAID/IRAQ 2008, 90).

These changes also have affected individual households. Whereas during the early relief and OFFP periods a teacher earned about US$20 monthly, by 2010 school teacher salaries had increased to US$300–510 (350,000–600,000 NID), physicians were making US$510–805 (600,000–950,000 NID), judges were earning up to US$850 (1,000,000 NID) while daily wages for unskilled laborers were $25 and skilled laborers earned $75 (see table 7). The KRG increased public-sector salaries again in January 2008 as a means of adjusting for inflation.[36] Others have

34. Interview with Dr. Saib Issa, director of statistics, KRG Council of Ministers, Arbil, Oct. 24, 2005. For example, because of the UN-INGO presence in Ainkawa, housing in Ainkawa has become a status symbol. Despite its majority Christian population, many new residents are Sunni Muslims who want to be close to the UN and international agencies.

35. Of the three cement factories in the Kurdistan Region, the Tasluja factory in Suleymaniya has been renovated in 2005 by the Orascum Construction Industries of Egypt. Production has increased from 300,000 tons per year (pre-2003) to a current production level of 2.3 million tons per year. Although the Serchinar factory will close operations, another cement factory at Bazian has been built by United Cement, an Egyptian firm, and produces 2.5 million tons per year. Additional cement factories are currently being planned or constructed in Arbil and Suleymania.

36. Goran interview; interview with Mr. Ahmad, Arbil, Nov. 13, 2007. Until 2007 the tax system in the Kurdistan Region was based on the old Iraqi system, with modifications made gradually.

TABLE 8. BASIC COMMODITY PRICES, ARBIL CITY (HAWLER),
SEPTEMBER 2007–MARCH 2010, IN NID (USD).[a]

Commodity	2007	2010
Beef (1kg)	10,000 (8.47)	12,000 (10.00)
Chicken (1kg)	3,500 (2.96)	3,500 (3.00)
Tomato (1kg)	500 (.42)	.750 (.65)
Cucumber (1kg)	500 (.42)	.750 (.65)
Tomato paste (1kg)	750 (.64)	1,500 (1.30)
Ahmad tea (1kg)	7,000 (5.90)	8,000 (6.80)
Vegetable oil (1kg)	2,250 (1.91)	2,500 (2.15)
Cooking oil (1L)	1,500 (1.28)	1,500 (1.28)
Sugar (1kg)	1,000 (8.50)	1,250 (1.06)
Fuel		
diesel (1L)	1,100 (.93)	900 (.76)
benzene (1L)	1,000 (.85)	950 (.81)
Housing		
land (250m²) purchase	90,000,000 (76,271)	180,000,000 (152,542)
house (per 1m³) purchase	250,000 (212)	500,000 (423)
monthly rent (2 rooms)	650,000 (551)	1,000,000 (847)

Source: Kurdistan Regional Government, Administration of Trade Monitoring, Arbil, 2007, and
local market.
[a]Exchange rate is 1,180 NID:US$1.

become millionaires overnight. In Zakho a former sheepherder established an
international trading business with China. A tea boy from Suleymaniya turned
looted metal scraps from Baghdad into a million-dollar rebar factory. According
to the Suleymaniya Chamber of Commerce, by 2006 Suleymaniya governorate
had about one thousand millionaires, mainly in Kelar, Chamchemal, and Kifry.
Another one thousand millionaires are estimated in Arbil.

For example, a modification was made in 1998 that imposed a tax on more than 600 meters of land
inside the cities. Personal property taxes also changed. Whereas a taxi driver had to pay a small tax
on his car if he sold it, after 2008 he became exempt, although taxes now apply to small cars and
pickups. Everyone had to pay a small tax on salaries before 1991, but after 2008 only those with a
university degree have to pay about 10 percent tax. The KRG's new tax law also adjusted taxes on
salaries while requiring residents to pay small property taxes.

Socioeconomic changes, alongside political openings made available in post-Saddam Iraq, have encouraged more complex forms of organization, including diverse civil society associations, youth and student groups, unions and syndicates, human rights activists and the media. By mid-2006, the Iraqi Kurdistan NGO Network (IKNN), an association that aims to expand NGO activities, had forty-three member organizations (Abdullah 2005, 173–79). Independent media sources such as *Hawlati, Awena, Xwendin-i Libral, Lvin,* and Radio Newa also have become popular outlets for disseminating alternative points of view. By 2008 *Hawlati* was the most distributed newspapers in the region, with a readership of eighteen thousand.

Opposition groups also have emerged as local populations have become aware of their individual and group rights (*maf*) (Rwanin 2006, 2; *Xwendin-i Libral* 2006, 3).[37] Ethnic and religious communities, including Hawremani, Ezidi, and Christian groups have demanded special autonomy within the Kurdistan Region. Youth groups have become the most vociferous opposition voices. Many recognize the corruptive practices of the political elites and the two main parties, and the gross discrepancies between the wealthy and the poor: those who can access the new shopping malls and those who cannot, and more simply, those with electricity and those without. Even though salaries have risen, price increases have posed new hardships for those dependent upon the PDS, as well as households affected by dollar-dinar exchange-rate fluctuations. Unchecked inflation, the near absence of domestic production, and emergence of a consumption culture has created a new community of working poor. By 2006, nearly 75 percent of families had two or three income sources: a primary job as a government employee and others as traders, taxis drivers, or merchants in the bazaar (ILCS 2005, 1:137). Inequalities shaped by changing socioeconomic structures and a political culture of *wasta* have drawn attention to the new upper class and their sense of privileges, while creating new social cleavages (Leca 1990, 155). *Peshmerga* cadres that spent a lifetime fighting for Kurdish nationalism have been excluded from benefits of development, living on a monthly salary of about 150,000 ID, or about US$128.

---

37. For instance, in May 2006 at the College of General Sciences, University of Salahaddin in Arbil, students demonstrated and demanded educational reforms and their individual rights. See *Rwanin* (2006) and *Xwendin-i Libral* (2006).

These trends have led to new forms of protest and mobilization. Many individuals have become highly critical of the KRG, apoliticized, or part of the opposition movement, which they see as a legitimate challenge to the two main secular nationalist parties. The Change Movement (Goran), led by the former PUK reform wing leader Nowsherwan Mustafa Amin, has posed the most important challenge to the KDP-PUK monopolization of power, and become particularly popular among young civil society workers and independent journalists and thinkers (such as Bakhtiar Ali, Rebin Herdi, Faroq Rafiq). Smaller parties have become part of the political opposition as well, which includes a combination of leftist and Islamic groups.[38] Instead of armed struggle for the Kurdish nation, these groups demand greater freedoms, services, educational reforms, human rights, and an end to political corruption.

Conclusions

Development opportunities created by the democracy mission, underlined by increased international recognition, enhanced the internal sovereignty of the Kurdish quasi-state and supported socioeconomic and political reforms. The most important change has been in the nature and scope of the aid program. The shift from short-term relief to capacity building and reconstruction provided the Kurdistan Region with the political authority and financial resources to advance development processes, which has encouraged a more complex political economy and society. Increasing diversification and open political spaces have unintentionally created new challenges to the KRG, mainly in the form of opposition movements and mobilizations "from below." Even then, these internal fragmentations have emerged as the rest of Iraq stagnated economically, limiting the interest of many Kurds in identifying with the weak Iraqi state.

38. For the July 2009 parliamentary and presidential elections in the Kurdistan Region, the four smaller parties—the Toilers Party, the Socialist Party, the Islamic Union, and the Islamic Society—merged to form their own opposition list, called the Services and Reform List (Khizmat u Chaksazi). After the election the socialist and leftist parties left the list and joined the Kurdistani List inside the Kurdish government.

5

Dependent Quasi-State

EMERGENT CLEAVAGES IN KURDISH SOCIETY may have shaken the traditional political establishment in the north; however, they have occurred while the rest of Iraq has stagnated economically and as important political issues remain unresolved between Arbil and Baghdad. With ongoing security problems in key Iraqi cities, and uninterrupted external patronage and international support to the Kurdistan Region, the KRG has continued to differentiate itself from other parts of the country. The Kurdistan Region has become "the Other Iraq." Even then, the processes that have helped create the Kurdish quasi-state have impeded its self-sustainability and independence. Aid conditionalities continue to assure the territorial integrity of Iraq and not the self-sufficiency of the Kurdistan Region. The federalist structure also has altered distribution modalities and established new administrative and financial linkages with Baghdad. This quasi-state condition of dependency and its related economic benefits, alongside ongoing domestic structural constraints, has created important incentives and demands for the Kurdistan Region to remain part of the Iraqi state.

Sustaining the Quasi-State

Like its emergent phase, the Kurdish quasi-state in post-Saddam Iraq has been sustained by external patronage, international support, and a weak central government. In addition to new rights and revenues provided to the KRG in the 2005 constitution, the aid program failed to establish an effective system of direction and coordination between the regions. Various organizations and offices assumed responsibility for the eighteen governorates in Iraq; however, they were unable to provide concerted action or mediate conflicts between regions and institutions (Herring and Rangwala 2006, 102–3). The U.S. government's emphasis on ethnic

103

and religious group quotas reinforced existing differences while creating new political and social dichotomies. Instead of moving away from communal interests toward a common purpose, or developing a sense of trust through shared cultural mechanisms, communities became increasingly focused on narrow group interests as a means of securing aid revenues from Baghdad (Reilly and Phillpot 2002, 917; Fukayama 1995, 10). For the Kurds, it meant having a "unified Kurdish voice" in Baghdad to lobby for Kurdish nationalist interests.

Consequently, institutional ties between regions remained virtually non-existent. Even when two of four of the ministers of industry in Baghdad were Kurds (Mohammed Towfiq and Fawzi Hawrimi), or Iraqi ministries had Kurdish deputy ministers, there was no real cooperation between the KRG and the Iraqi central government.[1] No joint committees or collaboration were systematically maintained between other ministries and sectors, such as health and education, resulting in the emergence of different systems in Arbil and Baghdad. Despite U.S. government–sponsored events and specific meetings between Kurdish and Iraqi officials, line ministries in Arbil and Baghdad continued to have no significant contact with one another.

Exclusionary conditions of membership in some Kurdish associations also have limited sociocultural linkages between the Kurdistan Region and the rest of Iraq. The union confederations of free trade in Kurdistan, for instance, oppose any formal ties with trade organizations in the rest of Iraq because of their Ba'athist heritage and administrative, financial, and organizational differences. The Kurdish Paralympics Committee, established in August 2005, has no relationship with the Iraqi Paralympics Committee. The Kurdistan Author's Union, created in the 1960s and once linked to the Iraqi's Author Association, narrowed its membership policies to exclude authors who have published anything against Kurdish nationalist interests. By 1996 the union refused 550 applications and had a membership of about 250 individuals (Awla 2003, 227–29).

Security issues have continued to impede potential cross-regional ties. The KRG's overriding concern for preventing the instability in southern and central Iraq from penetrating the Kurdistan Region has demanded a strict security environment, to include checks of non-Kurdish communities that have created

1. Taha Ismail Mohammed interview.

or helped intensify sentiments of distrust between Kurds and Arabs. Since the bombing of the al-Askari Mosque in Samarra in 2006, about thirty-eight thousand families have migrated to Suleymaniya province and fifteen thousand moved to Arbil, six hundred of which relocated to the Christian quarter of Ainkawa (USAID/IRAQ 2008, 27; Davis 2005).[2] Alongside enhanced security measures, internal migrations have added new pressures on local administrations to provide social services that identify communities by ethnicity and language. Arab migrants have not necessarily integrated into Kurdish schools, but rather, they have become part of various Arabic-language institutions established by the KRG for IDPs. Arabic-speaking professors that joined university faculties in the north have added valuable experience but also unintentionally have created tensions among students who do not know Arabic and are not interested in learning it.

Historical Legacies and Renewed Tensions

The sense of distinction between the Kurdish quasi-state and Iraq has been reinforced by an absence of political trust, just as it has been in previous periods. Despite legal mechanisms for power-sharing, a mutual commitment to federalism has not emerged. The KRG supports the 2005 constitution, while most Sunni Arab and Shi'a groups do not recognize its validity and seek to alter it. The strengthening of Arab nationalist and centralizing trends under former Iraqi prime minister Nuri al-Maliki, and the amassing of Kurdish *peshmerga* troops alongside sensitive border areas have heightened tensions between the KRG and the central government. In particular, these tensions have focused on budget allocations; disputed territories, including Kirkuk; and the hydrocarbons law.

For instance, while the 2005 Iraqi constitution grants the KRG an annual capital-investment budget of 17 percent of the federal budget (which, after deductions, reduces to about 13 percent), the KRG claims this amount is insufficient

2. Interview with Adil Botany, director of general security (Asaysh), Arbil, Mar. 27, 2007. Migrant families from southern and central Iraq are required to have a sponsor from the Kurdistan Region as a condition of temporary residence. Most are employed as goldsmiths, engineers, medical doctors, and professors. Another seven to eight thousand individuals have taken temporary residence as guest workers, which include daily workers from Mosul and foreign companies and their staff. These populations join Kurdish migrants from Iran, Turkey, and Syria.

and based on incorrect population percentages. Disagreements over the Kurds' fair share of the national budget and "who should pay what" are common and include the larger contention over Kurdish *peshmerga* forces.[3] The KRG argues that because the *peshmerga* are part of Iraqi forces, the central government should fund their salaries and activities apart from the KRG's 17 percent budget. Baghdad in turn, has refused and accuses the KRG of not paying its fair share of taxes due to the central government annually.[4] Even though the KRG has regulated previous payments, disagreements over revenue-sharing remain. Arbil and Baghdad also disagree about how to delineate Iraqi and Kurdish borders. The issue is based on who should control the disputed territories and the means by which they can be best secured. Since 2003 the Kurdish elites have applied their own strategies to reclaim and Kurdify disputed lands, which have antagonized the central government and non-Kurdish and minority communities. Immediately after the 2003 war, for instance, the KDP brought Kurds to the Ninevah Plains near Feshkabor and prevented Chaldo-Assyrian populations from returning to their homes (Olson 2005, 125). Makhmur, a largely Arab-populated town, has become mainly Kurdish.

Most important is Kirkuk, which has become a "periphery within a periphery" and part of competing power struggles between the central government, Arab groups, the KRG, and the government of Turkey (Chehabi 1997, 236). Open borders, de-Ba'athification processes, and land reclamations have encouraged voluntary and forced expulsions of Arabs from Kirkuk to southern and central Iraq and migration of Kurds back to the city. As part of the "normalization process,"

3. Interview with Nazar Jamil Abdul Aziz, adviser, Ministry of Martyrs and Anfal Affairs, KRG, Arbil, Apr. 19, 2009. For example, the KRG Ministry of Martyrs and Anfal Affairs planned a joint investment project for building a private hospital to service martyrs' families and agreed with Baghdad about an allocated budget. The central government then refused to pay, stating that it was a KRG project and that the KRG should use its portion of the national budget even if the hospital was to service all of Iraq.

4. Interview with Mohammad Ihsan, minister of extra-regional affairs, Paris, Aug. 2, 2006. In June 2006 Ihsan led a delegation to Baghdad to discuss the issue of financial allocations to the Kurdistan Region. Although the KRG was promised 17 percent of the total Iraqi income, in reality it only received 8.2 percent, for a loss of US$968,000,000. After months of tensions and negotiations, the Iraqi government agreed to return US$482 million to the KRG.

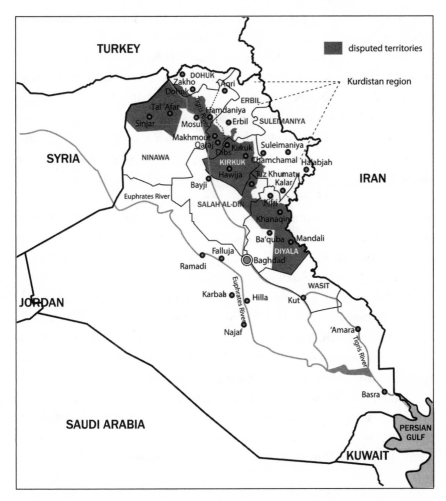

13. Map of the Kurdistan Region and disputed territories. Courtesy of International Crisis Group, Brussels.

the KRG has redistributed lands in Kirkuk for Kurds expelled by the former regime, resettled more than one hundred thousand Kurds to Kirkuk, compensated Arab settlers to return to their original homes, and promoted a mass-media campaign marketing Kirkuk as the "Jerusalem" and "Heart" of Kurdistan (Natali 2008; ICG 2006). The problem, however, is that the land distributions and other resettlement issues inside Kirkuk have been largely based on affiliations to the

KDP or PUK, which have reinforced the influence of the Kurdish political parties in the city.[5]

The re-Kurdification of Kirkuk has created imbalances in the distribution of power and new tensions between ethnic communities and Arbil and Baghdad. The first Kirkuk provincial council (Majlis-i Kirkuk) became the center of new disputes and the cause of ethnic tensions, particularly over council elections and equal distribution of high-level posts such as governor and chairman (Şwani 2002, 2).[6] For instance, to appease Arab and Turcoman communities that accused the Kurds of monopolizing power, Kurdish officials added ten representatives to the council from outlying areas and appointed non-Kurds to high-level positions on Kirkuk committees.[7] Arab and Turcoman representatives boycotted the council meetings, which were conducted in the Kurdish language. Intraparty conflicts also emerged between the PUK, the KDP, and the Kurdish list over council appointments (Natali 2008; Mohammed 2005, 243).

Kirkuk's influence on center-periphery relations also has been shaped by competing local communities. Most non-Kurdish populations have no commitment to article 140 (ICG 2006). Sunni Arabs regard Kirkuk and its oil revenues as part of Arab Iraq and not Kurdistan. Although Arab and Turcoman representatives returned to the Kirkuk council after an eighteen-month absence and have been promised a fairer distribution of local government positions, the balance of power is an unstable one. In May 2008 Arab political parties in Kirkuk formed a front with the objective of keeping Kirkuk outside the Kurdistan Region. The Turcoman Front, backed by Turkey, has threatened to boycott the future referendum

5. Interview with anonymous student resident of Kirkuk, Arbil, Mar. 11, 2008. The PUK concentrates its land distributions in the area between Chamchamal, Kirkuk, and Suleymaniya, while the KDP focuses on areas between Kirkuk and Arbil.

6. The distribution of seats was as follows: Iraqi Turcoman Front (8; includes 4 Turcoman parties and has 4 members in the Iraqi Parliament and 1 in the KRG), Turcoman Islamic Coalition (1), Iraqi National Assembly (1), Iraqi Republican Assembly (1), and Kirkuk Brotherhood List (26). Tasin Kahhiya, a Turcoman Shi'a, became president of the Kirkuk provincial council. He was replaced by Rizgar Ali, a Kurd, after the December 2005 election.

7. Interview with Mohammed Towfiq, Suleymaniya, May 16, 2008. In the first election, Kurds, Christians, and independents (five of whom were Kurds) aligned with each other. Ismail Hadidi and Irfan Kirkuki personally supported the Kurds, creating a pro-Kurdish bloc of twenty in the thirty-member council and upsetting the balance of power.

on Kirkuk. Further, although security problems are largely confined to the Arab-dominated areas of Hawija, Ansar al-Islam continues its attempts to penetrate the Kurdish areas of Kirkuk. Radical Shi'a communities supported by Moqtar al-Sadr groups have been encouraged to remain in Kirkuk and destabilize the region when necessary. Additional tensions are likely to reemerge between the Kurdish parties, who have fragmented among themselves over control of the city and its resources.

Baghdad has responded by calling for the creation of tribal councils in the disputed territories to challenge Kurdish influence, maintain order, and promote reconstruction.[8] The KRG has resisted this proposal, claiming that the councils are an extension of the central government's security forces in what they consider to be their territories. Local tensions have increased in certain areas over shifts in the balance of power, particularly after the January 2009 provincial council elections in which Sunni Arab groups gained greater influence in the political arena. In Mosul some Kurds have seen their representation in the provincial council decline as the al-Hadba list has assumed new posts and positions of authority. In April 2009 Kurdish communities in Sheikhan conducted public protests demanding to be part of the Kurdistan Region.

New disputes also have developed over exploiting and managing resources. Even though the KRG has passed its own hydrocarbons law and negotiated PSCs with European, American, and South Korean companies, the issue of who is administering and benefiting from oil remains a contentious one. To be sure, Kurdish officials recognize that even if Kirkuk becomes part of the Kurdistan Region, stipulations of the draft petroleum law indicate that Kirkuk's oil fields would not be part of the "yet to be discovered" oil wells that the KRG claims it can keep to itself, but rather, would fall under Baghdad's authority. Although the KRG regards the current and future oil discoveries as Iraqi oil and plans to deposit revenues from crude oil exports into a federal Iraqi account managed by the Iraqi State Oil Marketing Organization (SOMO), the central government still has not approved the PSCs.

---

8. Historically, these militias were able to co-opt and divide certain Kurds and maintain patronage networks; however, they had no real unifying force between the Kurdistan Region and Baghdad.

In fact, aside from deadlines on existing contracts, there still is no petroleum law or public agreement between the KRG and Baghdad on exporting petroleum to southern Iraq and Turkey. Iraqi oil minister Hussein al-Shahristani, concerned about Kurdish control of petroleum in the northern region, has rejected the KRG petroleum law, nullified the contracts, blacklisted all involved companies, and threatened to sanction the KRG. The KRG's oil minister, Ashti Hawrami, has ignored the threats, plans to sign additional contracts in the years ahead, and is preparing a new pipeline from Taq Taq to Zakho and an alternative means to export Kurdish crude from Iraq to the Cehan port in Turkey.[9] Underlying these efforts is the KRG's objective to attain economic autonomy. One Kurdish official clarified, "We know that the Baghdad government will stop funding us one day so we are making preparations with oil companies to establish an independent economy."[10]

More Constraints of Stalemate

Given the Kurdistan Region's differences with Baghdad, why has the KRG not attempted to separate from the weak Iraqi state? Alongside post–Gulf War development differentials and legacies of distrust, ethnic and political distinctions between the Kurdish North and Arab Iraq remained salient. After 2003 the Kurds created new discourses about the authenticity of their identity by differentiating themselves from Sunni and Arab populations.[11] They also disseminated new maps of the Kurdistan Region that included Kirkuk and the disputed territories as Kurdistani lands. Still, instead of seeking political independence, the KRG has compromised its nationalist agenda and become an integral part of a federal Iraq.

The survivability of the Kurdish quasi-state requires that it remain linked to Baghdad. Part of this condition can be attributed to the nature of the aid

9. Interview with Mohammed Amin, director-general, Ministry of Petroleum, KRG, Arbil, Nov. 27, 2007.

10. Ahmad interview. Other Kurdish informants have made similar comments.

11. Contemporary Kurdish discourses emphasize the authenticity of Kurdish identity as rooted in Zoroastrianism and Ezidism. Part of the new official discourse is that the Ezidis are the "purest and original Kurds."

regime, which has left the region weak and dependent. As in previous periods, the democracy mission ultimately has been committed to the reconstruction and development of a sovereign Iraqi state and not the Kurdistan Region. Lacking a real understanding of the regional distinctions of Iraq, or refusing to accept them, the U.S. government developed a contradictory policy of trying to decentralize power at the local levels and support Kurdish political and military forces as a means of stabilizing Iraq, while strengthening the central government (Tripp 2004, 548–55). It neither supported Kurdish autonomy in full nor attempted to establish an autonomous region.

Capacity building was encouraged, but to a point. Even though the KRG received generous revenues, was legitimized by the 2005 Iraqi constitution, and expanded its representation in Baghdad, it was excluded from key decision-making processes that impacted regional politics and development. From the outset donor coordination was organized between central government entities such as the Iraqi Strategic Review Board, the Iraqi Ministry of Planning, the Iraqi Ministry of Finance, the IRFFI, and recipient bodies, without the participation of KRG officials (UNSAI 2004, 17).[12] The one-Iraq policy also bound U.S.-funded projects and personnel in the Kurdistan Region to rigid Baghdad security rules, which wasted development funds that could have been used for reconstruction programs. Site visits by U.S. government personnel and affiliated contractors required private security contingents that often cost thousands of dollars daily. Despite increasingly apparent distinctions that emerged between the unstable central and southern regions and the Kurdish north, the policy of maintaining the status quo remained unchanged.

Consequently, international medical teams visited Baghdad to train Iraqi physicians, American specialists were seconded to Iraqi ministries, and national capacity-development programs focused on the central government without comparable programs in the Kurdish north. The training program for over 1,500 Iraqi police officers in Jordan had no Kurdish representation. Twenty police academies were funded for southern and central Iraq, but only two were supported in the Kurdistan Region. Of the eight U.S. border transition teams assembled for

12. Interview with Dilshad Mirani, Chief Coordinator, KRG Baghdad, Arbil, December 21, 2005.

the Kurdish north, only one was actually deployed (Chorev 2007). From 2003 to 2007 the Kurdish subcontracting company The Kar Group, implemented more than two hundred infrastructure projects in Iraq; however, none were conducted in the Kurdistan Region except for cleaning and trash collection.[13] In fact, aside from small water and sanitation projects, the democracy mission had no important investments or results to show in the Kurdish north. Although the U.S. Embassy in Baghdad eventually assumed CPA functions and helped establish four major centers to advise local governments and nineteen strategic areas targeted for U.S. funding, it established none in the three Kurdish governorates (Katzman 2005, 23).

Still, even if the external aid program expanded capacity building, structural constraints and political culture are likely to have impeded the Kurdish quasi-state's internal sovereignty and development potential, just as they did in previous periods. The bureaucracies of capital generation in the institutionally weak Kurdistan Region—absence of insurance, lack of transparency, inadequate capital reserves, and a dysfunctional banking system—hindered external investment, despite open borders and the incentives to invest. By 2008 the vast majority of new businesses in the Kurdistan Region were still family-run, while FDI was virtually nonexistent (USAID/IRAQ 2008, 90).[14] The emergent private sector in the Kurdish quasi-state also remained tainted by the policies of the past and the damage inflicted on the market and economy. Local populations increased their salaries but still have no confidence in public-sector institutions and continue to hoard their savings, which weakens the economy by taking money out of circulation.

Traditional sociopolitical structures continue to hinder political reforms. Attempts at decentralization have been imposed over a system and populations with limited understanding or experience with democracy. Real political power remains vested in the politburos composed of former party *peshmerga* believed to be the protectors of the real Kurdish nationalism. It is difficult for this influential group to transfer the power it has gained to others, particularly the youth, which

13. Barzinji interview, Jan. 13, 2007.

14. Abdulhalim interview, Jan. 3, 2008. In the Kurdistan Region the lines between FDI and joint venture projects are blurred. Most projects are funded by the KRG and subcontracted out to foreign companies.

undermines the potential for change. The parliament may have implemented a 30 percent quota for women and lowered the age for youth to participate; however, its members are selected by the political parties and are among the most conservative elements in Kurdish society. Despite what appears to be a representative legislature, the IKP still has limited authority and is not representative of the local populations that support reform.[15] In February 2010, members of the Goran movement, who secured twenty-five out of forty opposition seats in the IKP after the July 2009 parliamentary elections, walked out of the assembly in protest of violations of parliamentary rule and the limitations on free speech and their authority.

Nor have the Kurdish elites shown any interest in promoting real reform. Instead of attempting to break down traditional structures, they have strengthened them (Dube 1988, 2, 32). The unification agreement, which has dissipated with the aggrandizement of Barzani-KDP power and weakening of PUK influence, is essentially a back-door arrangement between the KDP and the PUK to guarantee that all power, resources, and revenues would be equally shared between them. Even though the opposition has called for transparency in the budget, the distribution of revenues by the KDP and PUK is not fully disclosed. Governors, ministers, and heads of directorates have no idea of KRG allocations once the budget arrives from Baghdad; it remains a private matter between the two main parties.[16] In addition, the two parties and their associated families have become the biggest landlords in the region, preventing the creation of individual property rights and a free market. Instead of moving toward greater political opening, the KRG has co-opted and controlled its challengers as a means of assuring stability and control.

For example, as in previous periods, the KRG has tried to pacify landowning classes by refusing to engage in land reform. Although the KRG canceled all land contracts issued by Saddam Hussein in the Kurdistan Region and assumed

15. Asaad interview. In 2007 the Kurdish parliament voted for a mixed presidential-parliamentarian system whereby the president of the Kurdistan Region would be elected directly by the people and not selected by the parliament. Although many members realized the danger of direct presidential elections, they could not challenge the power of the political parties.

16. Interview with Dana Ahmed Majid, former governor of Suleymania and current Goran representative, Dec. 1, 2007, Suleymaniya. Majid commented, "No one tells the parliament how much goes to the parties. Even the two parties agreed not to tell because they have too much to lose financially."

ownership of *miri* lands after 2003, it did not establish a system of individual property rights that could encourage entrepreneurship and efficient agricultural production. Rather, the KRG continues to lease out land on a contractual basis to individuals who specialize in agriculture and are interested in cultivation, or for industrial and personal use. Yet, without individual property rights, families have no land to construct houses legally in rural areas, and they risk arbitrary eviction (Mohammed and Ahmad 2007, 6). Further, ambiguous land records have made individual land ownership difficult to determine and have deterred investors from purchasing and developing properties, despite the opportunities to invest (USAID/IRAQ 2008, 42).

In fact, the vast wealth associated with the democracy mission has given the secular Kurdish nationalist parties even greater control of political processes and outcomes than in previous periods. Although the KRG has attempted to create an independent judicial system by establishing the Kurdistan Judicial Council (KJC) separate from the KRG Ministry of Justice (MOJ), the KDP and PUK still intervene in the selection of judges and determine legal outcomes (JRI-KS 2006).[17] The two parties control the local economy and business opportunities as well. Small and medium projects, such as supermarkets and shopping malls operate semi-independently; however, large-scale, financially lucrative projects are influenced by the KDP and PUK. Some claim there is no real free market in the Kurdistan Region, but rather, the same traditional families and private entrepreneurs control the market in a monopolistic way.

While calling for a decentralized Iraq, Kurdish officials have centralized the Kurdistan Region. Centralization trends have occurred alongside unresolved key issues with Baghdad, ongoing security problems, and growing Arab nationalist tendencies in parts of central and southern Iraq. In contrast to the OFFP period, wherein administration and governance was based at the provincial levels, after 2006 power became concentrated in Arbil in the institutions of the presidency and Council of Ministers. Both have assumed executive and legislative powers that in most democratic systems are delegated to the parliament or different branches of government, such as implementing laws and regulating the security and public monies of the Kurdistan Region. The Kurdistan Region's draft

---

17. Interview with Judge Salar Ahmed Abdul Aziz, Court of Cassation of Arbil, Apr. 11, 2007.

constitution, hastily passed through the IKP in June 2009 and waiting for final approval via a public referendum, encourages presidential rule at the expense of parliamentary rule.

Resistance to reform, and not insufficient aid monies, has hindered social change. The stubborn persistence of domestic structural constraints has challenged the expected outcomes of urbanization processes, and in particular, secularization and rationalization of authority structures. Urbanization may have encouraged structural differentiation and increased standards of living; however, it has not necessarily led to changes in social attitudes. Historical legacies continue to permeate Kurdish political culture and institutions. Despite the numerous conferences on educational reform, the public university system—from the selection of students to teaching methods to examinations—is still based on the Ba'athist system of secrecy and suspicion of outsiders. For instance, instead of welcoming diasporic Kurds and their expertise to the region, many high-ranking officials, staff, and teachers have alienated them and shunned their modernizing ideas. Social dichotomies have emerged between the diasporic returnees (*xariciyekan*) and local populations, which have created new cleavages in Kurdish politics and society between the reformers and those attempting to protect the existing system.

Similarly, despite efforts by KRG education officials to increase literacy rates by promoting school construction in all villages, districts, and cities of the Kurdistan Region, some localities have resisted. In one situation, the village mufti, concerned about losing potential sheep herders and traders, refused the schools and demanded mosques instead.[18] This attitude is endemic throughout parts of Dohuk governorate, which, despite being one of the wealthiest areas in the Kurdistan Region, still has high illiteracy rates. By 2004 about 50 percent of the province's population was unable to read a newspaper or write a short letter (ILCS 2004, 1:85–97).

In other regions, urbanization actually strengthened conservative values and created new tensions between communities. In Suleymaniya city, often referred

18. Interview with Foy Hartman, retired U.S. military intelligence officer and current managing director, North Star Security Company, Suleymaniya, Dec. 5, 2007. This same mufti also refused water distributions from U.S. military officers unless he could distribute the water to the villagers himself.

to the intellectual and cultural capital of the Kurdistan Region, the mass out-migration of city dwellers to Europe and the influx of rural communities into the city over the past two decades has created both modernization trends and a villagization of the city. In the upper-class Azadi neighborhood, where million-dollar villas have been constructed by migrant village families, in some cases to house two wives, traditional values clash with the open attitudes of secular communities. Some argue that the situation for women has actually deteriorated, with teenage marriages, divorces, and polygamy at a record high. New forms of wealth have given men the resources to marry young, uneducated girls by paying a larger dowry or to purchase second wives. Further, despite harsher penalties, honor killing and female genital mutilation against women and young girls, as well as other forms of symbolic violence and discrimination, is rampant in the region (Fischer-Tahir 2009; Taysi 2009).[19]

Traditional norms also continue to prevent the creation of positive social capital beyond the family unit (Reilly and Phillpot 2002, 925). Localist and tribal affiliations and a dichotomy between strong families and a centralized political apparatus have left marginal room for intermediate social groups to take form. Modernization processes have weakened these ties while replacing others with new forms of patronage (Thörlind 2000, 17; Collier 2002, 35–36; Berman 2001, 37; Encarnacion 2003, 10–11; Hooghe and Stolle 2003, 5). Absence of social capital and weak political institutions, in turn, has limited the ability of an independent civil society to develop and be sustained (Collier 2002, 34; Grootaert and van Bastelaer 2002, 3). Although various associational groups have emerged, the number of independent, community-based associations is small, representing about 5 percent of the total civil groups in the Kurdistan Region. The vast majority of associational groups and political parties are financed and licensed by the KRG and the Ministry of the Interior. The KRG and its party apparatus—the KDP and the PUK—provide monthly stipends, loans, land, and job opportunities to students and certain unions, such as the journalists, students, teachers, engineers, and lawyers' associa-

19. Interview with Ms. Sazgar, chief of the Prosecution Office, KRG, Ministry of Justice, Arbil, Apr. 11, 2007. There is also an absence of female judges, which represent only 1.9 percent of a total of 156 judges in the Kurdistan Region.

14. Civil society demonstrations in the Kurdistan Region, ca. 2007. Photograph courtesy of the *Kurdish Globe,* Arbil.

tions.[20] The Kurdistan teachers' union, with some 35,000 members, has elected its board members according to political party lists and not on an individual basis (Awla 2003, 235–36, 242). The parties also control and repress independent forms of expression perceived as threats to its power, regional stability, and the strategic agreement.[21]

20. The KDP student and youth wings are the Kurdistan Student Union and the Union of the Democratic Youth of Kurdistan respectively. The PUK-backed student and youth groups are the Kurdistan Student Association, the Freedom Youth Union of Kurdistan, and Solidarity. The youth branch of the Kurdistan Islamic Union (KIU) is the Kurdistan Student Development Organization. Most identify as "independent."

21. For example, in August 2006, independent newspapers announced a planned demonstration in Suleymaniya city against the lack of services. At the same time, the PUK security policy announced the capture of more than 200 individuals of Arab origin, many of whom were from Syria. This security alert discouraged people from participating in the demonstration because they feared real terrorist acts, as well as retaliatory violence from the KRG and political parties. According to the independent press, *Hawlati* and *Awena,* more than 1,000 people attended the demonstration in

For example, despite the IKP's ratification of a media law in 2009 to expand media rights and individual expression ("Projey-i yasa-i kari rojnameynusî ley Kurdistan"), local newspapers often reveal independent journalists who have been arrested or "interviewed" by the Kurdish security police. Independent presses are brought to court and punished with heavy fines for printing or reproducing articles considered insulting to the political elites (Committee to Protect Journalists 2009).[22] Some journalists have disappeared, been arrested, and even been killed for crossing the "red line."[23]

Nor have the two main parties been particularly tolerant of the opposition movement. Even though opposition parties won 40 seats in the 111-seat IKP in July 2009, which activated the parliament, serious restrictions remain on political freedoms.[24] In response to an overly critical opposition, the KRG has banned the independent media and placed plain-clothes security police inside

---

Suleymaniya city (also demonstrations in Sharezur and Kalar), and about 200 people were arrested. The authorities used the incident to impose further restrictions against civil society elements in behalf of the KRG's "national security interests."

22. In March 2009, the independent newspaper *Hawlati* was fined US$8,653 (10,000,000 NID) and the former editor-in-chief, Abid Aref, was fined US$2,590 (3,000,000 NID) for publishing a translated article that criticized the Iraqi president and Kurdish leader Jelal Talabani. Local populations in Suleymaniya, incensed by the conclusions of the court, raised money for the newspaper and paid the fines. In another incident on February 4, 2009, Shwan Mohammed, the former editor-in-chief of the independent newspaper *Awena,* was fined US$2,590 for publishing an anonymous article that defamed a Kurdish tribal leader.

23. A journalist can cross the red line by: (1) criticizing the Barzani or Talabani families; (2) monitoring the money trail, including making unsubstantiated corruption charges against individuals; or (3) discussing certain beliefs or writing about the Prophet or the Qur'an. On July 21, 2008, twenty-three-year-old Soran Mama Hama, an investigative reporter for *Lvin* journal, was assassinated in front of his parents' home in Kirkuk, allegedly because of an article he was writing about the involvement of Kurdish officials in prostitution rings in Kirkuk (ICG 2010).

24. Twenty-four lists competed for the parliamentary seats and five individuals for the presidency. Voter outcome was 78 percent of over two million eligible voters. Although the election was declared relatively free and fair, opposition groups complained about election fraud. Many individuals could not vote, while others voted multiple times. The Change (Goran) list offices in Arbil were ransacked while outbreaks of violence occurred in Suleymaniya between members of different lists. Ma'soud Barzani also called a press conference in one polling station during the elections, which violated election procedures. Barzani received over 78 percent of the votes and won the presidency.

the parliament. Threats and intimidation against Goran continued throughout the March 2010 election campaign for the Baghdad parliament. Goran members were harassed, attacked, and killed, and their offices were ransacked in certain areas of Suleymaniya province, without any investigation by government officials. Attacks against Islamic groups also occurred in Dohuk province, further underlining the weak institutions in the Kurdistan Region and the risks involved in challenging the traditional Kurdish political establishment.

Between Arbil and Baghdad

The dependent and institutionally weak nature of the Kurdish quasi-state, alongside the political demands of the federalist structure, has necessitated compromises with Baghdad. Despite years of disagreement, the KRG sent Kurdish *peshmerga* forces to Baghdad as part of the Iraqi national forces and eventually agreed to raise the new Iraqi flag in the region next to the Kurdish flag. The Kurdish elite also were persuaded by their American patron to compromise on the number of seats that the Kurdistan Region would receive in the Baghdad parliament after the 2010 elections, despite criticisms by Kurds that the number was disproportionately low (ICG report 2010, 19–24).

The Kurds' need to remain part of Iraq has been reinforced by economic realities and the KRG's overriding development objectives. Changes in distribution modalities and absence of alternative revenue sources inside the region have created new dependencies on the central government and external actors. The Kurdish north may have realized a US$3,500 per capita income in 2008; however, this income represented 95 percent of the KRG budget from Baghdad, and in particular, sales of Iraqi oil revenues (Pollack 2008, 8). An important component of the KRG budget includes the PDS, which plays a key role in balancing families' household economies and that 25 percent of the poorest populations in the Kurdistan depend upon for their subsistence (FAO 2003). The KRG further depends upon the central government to pay the salaries of its ministers and certain judges linked to the Cassation Court for property disputes in Baghdad.[25]

---

25. Judge Aziz interview. The special Baghdad-based Cassation Court for Property Disputes, created in 2003, has branches in all cities of the Kurdistan Region. Two of the seven judges in the Cassation Court in Baghdad are Kurdish. The court is separate from the KRG Ministry of Justice,

15. Iraqi and Kurdish flags. Photograph courtesy of Ali Ayverdi.

Consequently, when the central government did not pay Arbil its due share of the 2008 budget on time, contractors and *peshmerga* in the Kurdish north went unpaid for months. This delay forced some companies to close operations temporarily and instigated public discontent.

In addition, as in the prewar and early relief periods, the uneven distribution of resources in post-Saddam Iraq requires compromises by Iraqi Kurds, who must choose between basic needs and independence. Even though the KRG has constructed power lines from Dohuk to Arbil, which reduces dependency on Mosul governorate, it still receives and provides water and electricity to Baghdad, while depending upon Turkey to meet additional electricity demands. The

and its judges are employed by Baghdad and implement federal law regarding property in the Kurdistan Region. Indeed, the federal court in Baghdad, created by the 2005 Iraqi constitution, has no jurisdiction in the Kurdistan Region, and the security situation and divisions between the Kurdistan Region and Baghdad warrants against Kurds bringing their cases to Baghdad for an appeal. However, legally, someone from the north can take recourse through the federal court if a decision made by a judge is against the Iraqi constitution.

KRG Ministry of Electricity often negotiates with Baghdad to get the region's fair allocation of power, which is based on the seasonal flow of dam water. In return for keeping the dam gates open and letting water flow freely to southern and central Iraq for irrigation, the KRG receives a small amount of electricity from the central government.[26]

Commercial opportunities have revived old linkages and created new ones between the Kurdistan Region and the rest of Iraq. Open borders and the quest to satisfy the larger Iraqi market have made the Kurdistan Region a vital link and a gateway to Iraq as a whole. Kurdish businessmen travel to Baghdad and Basra for commercial purposes and have signed food- and construction-importing contracts with international companies. Populations from central and southern Iraq work in the Kurdistan Region, where well-paid jobs and secure living conditions are available. About 80 percent of the contractors of the Ramadi areas dealing in cars are working in Suleymaniya.[27] Similarly, commercial relationships between Dohuk and Mosul provinces have not ruptured but reversed since the prewar and early relief periods. Whereas Kurds once migrated to Mosul province for better education, services, and business opportunities, since 2006 Arab and Kurdish families from Mosul have take refuge in Dohuk, where personal security and employment opportunities are available. Dohuk governorate has become an important supplier to Mosul and focuses on Baghdad for expanding future business and marketing activities. Kurdish chambers of commerce encourage wealthy Iraqi businessmen in Jordan and Syria to invest in the Kurdistan Region "because it is Iraq."[28] In 2006 the Warka Bank, established by the Boniya family from Baghdad, created branches in all three Kurdish governorates.

The intertwining of capital relations between the KRG and regional states also has demanded political concessions for economic gain. To be sure, increasing tensions over the PKK and Pejak, the Iranian Kurdish dissident group based in the Iraqi Kurdish border region, as well as the arrest of an Iranian Qods officer in Suleymaniya in 2008, caused the temporary closings of Turkish airspace and Turkish and Iranian border points. These incidents directly impacted the Kurdistan Region's economy and, in some cases, cost the KRG up to US$1 million daily

26. Barzinji interview, Jan. 13, 2007.
27. Mirza interview.
28. Abdulhalim interview, Jan. 3, 2008.

16. Kurdistan Region at the crossroads of Iraq, ca. 2008. Photograph courtesy of Ali Ayverdi.

in lost revenue (*Hawlati* 2007a). Instead of defending pan-Kurdish nationalism or engaging in armed conflict with cross-border Kurdish nationalist groups, the KRG has pursued a strategy of cooperation with regional governments to assure external patronage, international recognition, and open borders. In 2009, with pressure from regional states, Baghdad, and foreign governments, it closed PKK-affiliated offices in the cities, blockaded routes to the Qandil Mountains where the PKK is based, and adopted a public position against PKK activities. Similarly, as part of their "gentleman's agreement" with the Iranian government, Suleymaniya officials promised to control Iranian Kurdish dissident activity in return for open borders to the province.

Cross-regional cultural ties continue or have been reestablished between different communities. Despite security challenges, lawyers, journalists, students, scholars, poets, artists, and sports groups from around the country and the region convene in the Kurdish north for art expositions, music festivals, conferences, and events. The international conference on Higher Educational Reform in Iraq, organized by groups in Baghdad, Arbil, and Europe in December 2007, was conducted in Arbil in the Arabic, Kurdish, and English languages. In March 2008 the KRG hosted the Arab League conference in Arbil, assembling the world's leading Arab delegations in the Kurdish capital city. The Iraqi National Orchestra plays regularly in Suleymaniya, bringing together musicians from all parts of Iraq in a common forum.

Linguistic ties also remain. The majority of young Kurds may not know the Arabic language; however, the larger Kurdish community is still bound to it for political, business, religious, and personal reasons. Many of the growing number of high-quality hotels and professional institutions in the Kurdistan Region employ Arabic and English as the language of communication and instruction, alongside Kurdish. The Iraqi constitution and official correspondences between Arbil and Baghdad are written in the Arabic language and translated into Kurdish and at times, English.[29] In 2008 the KRG parliament building added Arabic to its Kurdish and English insignia, underlining the ongoing importance of the Arabic language in the Kurdistan Region.

Similarly, in Arbil and other towns and cities in the Kurdistan Region, Arabic is used in the mosques and for Islamic holidays and events. University students are required to learn Arabic for advanced studies in law and Islamic jurisprudence. Chaldo-Assyrians from Mosul, Baghdad, and Basra areas participate in conferences and activities sponsored by Arabic-speaking Christian groups in the Kurdistan Region. During the visit of the archbishop in May 2006, dozens of Christian communities throughout Iraq traveled to Ainkawa, the Christian quarter in Arbil. Moreover, despite the difficulties of integration, the presence of Arab communities in Kurdish-populated neighborhoods also has helped break down social and political stereotypes, particularly among the young. Many have indicated their preference for living in a peaceful and prosperous federal Iraqi state and not necessarily in an independent and isolated Kurdistan.[30]

29. The issue of the language to be used in writing the constitution of the Kurdistan Region has been one of many sources of tension between members of the Kurdish commission to prepare the constitution. The main contention was between Nuri Talabani, who had prepared a version in the Kurdish language, and the head of the committee, Firsat Ahmed, who argued that there was no scientific Kurdish language. Others have argued that some combination of both Kurdish dialects should be used, and not just the Sorani dialect. See "Ley kobuneweyekî na asayi 15 madey bô reshnusî destur ziad krawa," *Cemawar*, Apr. 2, 2007, 1, 12.

30. Preliminary findings from a youth-attitudes survey conducted by the author in spring and fall 2009 in five universities in the Kurdistan Region. When asked "How would you like to see the

Kurds living outside the Kurdistan Region or in provinces neighboring Arab-majority populations also have crossed sectarian boundaries. Approximately 655,000 Kurds living in Baghdad, mainly Shi'a (Faili), remain linked to Arab communities and have little support for the KRG or Kurdish nationalist parties.[31] Some Shabak communities (Shi'a Kurds) in Mosul have developed political relationships with Arab Shi'as as a means of countering Kurdish nationalist political parties. In preparing for the provincial council elections in 2008, leading Sunni Kurdish tribal communities in Mosul such as the Herchis, Serchis, and Zibaris turned to Sunni Arab groups to form a block against the Kurdish nationalist parties.

Even if all Kurdish communities mobilized in behalf of Kurdish nationalism and had a unified Kurdish voice in Baghdad, the Kurdistan Region would remain bound to Iraq by international law and regional politics. Foreign governments are ready to export food and materials, and businesses are active in soliciting bids from the KRG. Still, foreign investors are generally wary of doing business in the Kurdistan Region, where contracts are not legally binding and there is no rule of law (Kolsto 2006, 729). Small- to medium-sized oil companies may have invested in the Kurdistan Region; however, the major international petroleum companies have refused, despite the relatively secure environment and attractive investment law. Until the Kurdistan Region receives de jure status or Kurdish autonomy is institutionalized in a federal Iraq, large-scale international business contracts are likely to be negotiated through the central government in Baghdad, and not the KRG in Arbil.

The petroleum sector is particularly sensitive to the legal and political relations that unfold between Arbil and Baghdad. Despite the KRG's perceived rights to negotiate oil contracts in the region, the possibilities of developing an independent Kurdish economy are compromised by the highly politicized nature of petroleum. The situation of the landlocked region and the logistics of transporting petroleum out of Iraq demand compromises with the Iraqi central government and Turkey over oil exploration, revenue-sharing, pipeline tariff income,

---

Kurdistan Region and Iraq in 15 years?" about half of the interviewees (age 18–25) indicated their preferences for a federal Iraq while the other half wanted an independent Kurdistan.

31. Interview with Qubad Talabani, KRG representative, Washington D.C., Aug. 9, 2006. During the 2005 parliamentary elections, only 25,000 members of this group voted for the Kurdistan list.

and Kurdish autonomy. Even though Baghdad eventually authorized the expor-tation of Kurdish crude from two northern fields on June 1, 2009, there still is no mutually agreed upon hydrocarbons law or mechanism in which the KRG can officially and regularly pay oil companies. Some companies have temporarily closed their wells, suspended operations, and may leave the region for nonpay-ment of costs.[32]

Turkey also remains wary of an increasingly autonomous Kurdistan and to the KRG assuming jurisdiction over Kirkuk and its petroleum revenues. Although official meetings between Turkish diplomats and KRG leaders commenced in early 2008 as part of a new official dialogue that includes discussing the PKK, and the Turkish government established a consulate in Arbil in February 2010, sensi-tive issues over petroleum and the status of Kirkuk remain unresolved. Turkey has stated that it will thus far negotiate only with Baghdad regarding petroleum and pipeline revenues, further undermining the political maneuverability of the KRG and its autonomy apart from Iraq. Consequently, while Baghdad has lim-ited direct authority in the Kurdistan Region, it has become the link between the KRG and Turkey. Kurdish officials have suggested the creation of a High Council for Petroleum to supervise all oil fields in Iraq, which would still require direct coordination and ongoing linkages between Arbil and Baghdad.

Conclusions

The very nature of the democracy mission has assured that the Kurdistan Region will remain part of a federal Iraq and that it will not become "too autonomous."

---

32. Since oil exportations commenced on June 1, 2009, the Norwegian Company DNO Inter-national ASA and the Turkish company TTOPCO have not been paid by the KRG. Both companies stopped exporting crude oil in October 2009 for nonpayment. Instead, they capped their wells or are using "topping units" (asphalt plants) to replace a refinery and then selling the poor quality crude to local merchants, who are illegally transporting it by trucks to Turkey and Iran at a dis-counted rate of less than US$40 per barrel. Crescent Oil, which sends gas to local power stations, has not received payment since October 2008 and is owed US$130 million by the KRG. A "ques-tionable" trading deal arranged by Ashti Hawrami and DNO, in which Hawrami purchased 4.8 percent of DNO shares at US$30 million, caused the suspension of DNO operations for two weeks. The issue of how the KRG is going to pay the oil companies remains an important one.

Instead of being a highly autonomous region, the Kurdish quasi-state has stagnated between development and dependency. This condition of dependency and the need for ongoing capacity building has created new priorities for the Kurdish quasi-state based on economic development and stability. In contrast to previous periods, protecting Kurdish interests in post-Saddam Iraq requires maintaining open borders for commercial benefits, assuring external patronage for recognition, and guaranteeing international support for ongoing legitimacy and necessary resources. These objectives have reconfigured the Kurdish nationalist agenda, created new demands for negotiation with the central government, and compromised the notion of a Kurdistan Region apart from Iraq.

Conclusions

Sustaining the Kurdish Quasi-State

THIS DETAILED CASE STUDY reveals that the transition of the unrecognized Kurdistan Region to a quasi-state is more complex than symbolic nation building or the will of the people to be apart from the central government. Rather, it is a by-product of international aid of which the "benefits of stalemate" are derived—recognition, legitimacy, and development. External aid channeled to Iraqi Kurds after the 1990 Persian Gulf War as victims of Saddam Hussein opened avenues for economic recovery, reconstruction, and reform. Security assistance has been an essential component of this support because it helped create an environment of relative stability in which humanitarian aid and future development programs could be implemented.

The trajectory of the Kurdish quasi-state further indicates that it is not only the presence of external aid but its continuity over time that can encourage post-conflict recovery and rehabilitation. Each phase of the aid program has built upon previous periods and provided the groundwork for current development processes. Short-term relief assistance of the first aid period helped alleviate immediate post-conflict needs, resettle populations, and build new political institutions. A more expansive aid regime during the OFFP period, alongside sustained security assistance, played a key role in mediating conflict and encouraging ongoing stability, confidence building, income generation, and entrepreneurship. Personal wealth generated during the OFFP period became the impetus for the hotels, supermarkets, and modern buildings constructed in the Kurdistan Region after 2003. Long-term infrastructure development in post-Saddam Iraq could not have emerged without this economic foundation, as well as liberalization policies and mechanisms for regional autonomy. Had international support for the Kurds been interrupted during any one of these phases, the spoils of peace in the Kurdistan Region may not necessarily have taken their current form.

The key juncture in the Kurdish quasi-state trajectory was 2003. The democracy mission altered the nature of the aid regime and its related opportunity structures by moving away from food and fuel handouts and focusing on capacity building. One of the most significant transformations has been in the regional economy. Commercial exchanges that had minimal impact on the Kurdish transit zone in the prewar period have become an important source of income generation. The very foundations of the Kurdish quasi-state economy have shifted from smuggling to official multi-million-dollar cross-regional trade. Lucrative and complex commercial relations, in turn, have created interdependencies with regional states, particularly Turkey, which has become the major exporter of consumer and luxury goods in the region. Turkish companies, and the military generals who own them, are now directly involved in large-scale construction projects that have been vital to the reconstruction and rehabilitation of the region.

A more complex and integrated economy linked to international markets has supported sociopolitical changes as well. Modernization and urbanization trends that were once confined to Baghdad in the prewar period have reached the Kurdistan Region. Few Iraqi Kurds today live in the villages, weave carpets, or engage in agricultural work like their parents did. With more than half the local populations under the age of twenty-five, most have become part of young, educated cadres seeking jobs, higher wages, educational opportunities, and a better way of life in the city centers. Many young populations also continue to their efforts to leave their region, often illegally, to realize a better life in Europe.

Urbanization and development processes, however, have been incomplete and uneven, causing new tensions within Kurdish society and politics. Gross discrepancies in wealth have created or reinforced dichotomies between the rich and the poor. Local populations, especially the youth, have responded to these socioeconomic differentials and the conspicuous consumption of the political elites by engaging in new forms of protest. Instead of fighting in the mountains on behalf of the Kurdish nation as their parents did, they have become highly critical of the KRG and the Kurdish political parties, while retaining their sense of Kurdish identity. Many have joined the opposition movement as a way of mobilizing against the government and the traditional party establishment.

Despite these political challenges, open spaces encouraged by aid programs have had unintended consequences on the Kurdish national agenda. Kurdish elites have taken advantage of international support by Kurdifying education systems, histories, the media, and territories, which has challenged existing boundaries and created new ones. As recognition and resources for the KRG increased over time, so too did its internal sovereignty and leverage in Iraq, particularly as the central government remained weak and unstable. The KRG capitalized on its perceived, although unclear, rights accorded by the 2005 Iraqi Constitution by negotiating a hydrocarbons law and PSCs for the region, initiating private-sector investment, and sending representatives abroad to discuss commercial and political affairs. The KRG now regularly receives world leaders, congressional delegations, and UN missions—all of which have strengthened its international recognition and legitimacy outside Iraqi borders.

These developments occurred while parts of southern and central Iraq stagnated economically and remained politically unstable, which reinforced the KRG's desire to differentiate itself from the rest of the country. The aid program encouraged this rift. U.S. efforts to fill ethnic and religious group quotas, tolerate Kurdish monopolization of power in Kirkuk city, and integrate some former Ba'athists into the police forces supported the resurgence of ethnic and religious identities in the Kurdistan Region and disputed territories, particularly Kirkuk. Baghdad's refusal to implement key articles of the 2005 Iraqi constitution, its failure to accept real power-sharing, and its centralizing trends further heightened tensions between the Kurds and the central government.

Indeed, historical memories continue to play a key role in defining territories and political identities, and the relationship that could be carved between Arbil and Baghdad. Most Kurds may be committed to federalism; however, they are hostile to maintaining a status quo that represents years of what they perceive is Arabization and a violation of Kurdish honor, which is rooted in the land. Despite the economic and financial opportunities made available in the Kurdistan Region after 2003, local populations and political elites still consider themselves Kurds first and have little or no sense of shared Iraqiness.

It can be argued that the emergence of and transformations in the Kurdish quasi-state could have occurred without humanitarian aid. The termination of the international sanctions regime and the internal embargo against the Kurdistan Region in 2003 was essential to opening borders and permitting legal trade.

Kurdish entrepreneurs were likely to have engaged in expansive economic activities anyway and to have developed interdependent commercial relations with Turkey and regional states. The region had served as a transit zone well before the arrival of aid in 1992 and continued to maintain that role during each aid program, although as part of an underground economy. Urbanization processes also had been ongoing since the 1990s, with greater attention to education and modernizing city centers. Thus, Kurdish nationalism could have flourished without external aid, just as it did under successive Iraqi authoritarian regimes.

Yet, without the external patronage and international support linked to aid missions to the KRG, the benefits of foreign assistance may not necessarily have reached or remained in the Kurdistan Region. For instance, development differentials that emerged in Iraq during the prewar period were a consequence of an imbalanced distribution of resources that favored the central and southern regions. In the absence of international support or mechanisms for power and revenue sharing between Baghdad and the outlying regions, the Kurdistan Region had no access to or control of resources within its territorial boundaries. It was only with the implementation of humanitarian aid in 1992, creation of a safe haven, checks placed on the Iraqi Ba'athist government, and the eventual shift from short-term relief to capacity building that long-term development could commence, and with it, the emergence of the Kurdish quasi-state.

Policy Implications

If external aid has empowered the Kurdish quasi-state, it also has checked its self-sustainability. Despite the image of a "booming" and self-reliant Kurdistan Region, the reality indicates a condition of weakness and dependency. Even with the commitment to capacity building after 2003, donor organizations, international law, and regional politics continued to emphasize the territorial integrity of Iraq and not the self-sufficiency of the Kurdistan Region. In fact, as the Kurdish quasi-state gained greater political autonomy, regional states with Kurdish populations of their own became increasingly engaged in checking its power, although discreetly. Despite expanded commercial ties and improved political relations with Arbil, the government of Turkey still refers to the KRG as "the local administration in northern Iraq." Turkey and Iran also control borders to the landlocked region and have caused important financial losses to the KRG and local merchants by suspending air flights, closing the border to commercial traffic, or engaging in cross-border military incursions.

Most important is the Kirkuk issue, whose potential negotiation has been stifled not only by the Iraqi central government and Iraqi Kurds, but also by regional states and local non-Kurdish communities concerned about an economically autonomous and politically independent Kurdistan. The Kurds made have won six seats for Kirkuk in the March 2010 Iraqi parliamentary elections, but they are still faced with significant challenges to negotiating a solution to ownership of the province. The politics of petroleum in Iraq, the key role of the sovereignty regime, and the need for ongoing international recognition will require that the Kurds make continued concessions on Kirkuk, particularly if they want to export petroleum, pay the oil companies, and attract future investment in the region.

Thus, even if regional states supported a highly autonomous Kurdistan Region, the KRG would need to remain attached to post-Saddam Iraq for its political and economic survival. Although there is no direct correlation between foreign assistance and center-periphery relations, this case study shows that the post-Saddam aid program, and in particular, the federalist project, has shifted distribution modalities and created new demands for political compromise and cooperation. KRG officials may have Kurdified the education system, media, territorial boundaries, and social spaces; however, they have had to resituate Kurdish nationalism within the larger Iraqi state. The benefits of stalemate have been generous enough and vital to the survivability of the Kurdistan Region to encourage this sort of compromise. To be sure, the short-term nature of external aid during the first two periods alleviated immediate needs, permitted rehabilitation, and encouraged Kurdish autonomy but left the region marginalized from the national and world economies. With no official recognition, vested interest or legitimacy in the country, the KRG had no reason to negotiate with the central government or remain part of the Iraqi state. The relationship between Arbil and Baghdad was largely based on conflict.

As the KRG's recognition, leverage, and legitimacy in a federal Iraq strengthened, so too did the opportunities and need to negotiate with the central government. Whereas political decisions were once made as part of secret deals between Kurdish tribal leaders and Iraqi officials, after 2003 they became part of open parliamentary and constitutional processes. Instead of threatening to blow up

Iraqi pipelines like they did in the 1960s, Kurdish officials can now legally challenge Baghdad for failing to comply with key issues of the Iraqi constitution. The KRG also can pressure the central government to negotiate Kirkuk and the disputed territories, reallocate the national budget, and recognize its rights to exploit and manage natural resources in the region.

These findings have implications for the future of the Kurdish quasi-state and its place in Iraq. While some Kurdish nationalists, scholars, and policy-makers argue for, or fear the eventual territorial separation of the Kurdistan Region from the rest of the country, a deeper look at the nature of the Kurdish quasi-state reveals otherwise. That is, despite regional and ethnic distinctions that have become salient since 2003, the Kurdistan Region cannot develop and prosper without remaining part of Iraq and cooperating with neighboring states. Alongside continued international recognition, legitimacy, and support, the benefits of political stalemate include 17 percent of the budget from Baghdad, multi-million-dollar investment projects, and ongoing commercial ties with neighboring states, all of which require that borders to the landlocked region remain open. With the vast majority of exports to Iraq passing through the Kurdish transit zone, the Turkish-Iraqi Kurdish border area remains vital to sustaining the landlocked Kurdistan regional economy. Fully aware of the key role Turkey has in its political economy, KRG officials have made significant compromises on Kurdish nationalism and will likely to make additional ones in the future, to ensure a viable trade zone for international investors, the exportation of Kurdish crude, and potential pipeline revenues.

The Kurdish quasi-state also remains linked to Iraq in less obvious ways. Although tensions continue at the elite level between Arbil and Baghdad, important relationships exist and have developed among local communities that cross ethnic and sectarian lines. Arab populations that migrated to the Kurdistan Region after 2006 work and live among Arabic-speaking Kurdish communities in the north. Christian communities—Kurds and Arabs—that have been persecuted throughout Iraq have come together in Arbil in a shared sense of victimization and mutual support. Kurds who have spent a lifetime in Baghdad and Mosul are more attached to people and places in central Iraq than to those in the Kurdistan Region. Local populations who have never interacted with Arab communities also have realized a shared sense of victimization and have assisted Arab refugee communities in the north. Some internally displaced Arabs complain about discrimination in the north and plan to return to their homes in Baghdad if and when the security situation improves. Others have gained a new appreciation for their Kurdish hosts and the relative security they have in the north. Cultural, commercial, and linguistic ties between Arabs and Kurds continue to challenge the notion of an Iraq divided along sectarian lines: Kurds, Shi'as, and Sunni Arabs.

These dependencies and interactions reveal that external assistance can play a key role in shaping behavior and political outcomes in the Kurdistan Region. Foreign governments and organizations should take greater advantage of this condition of weakness and press the KRG to conform to international standards and practices, particularly relating to human rights, good governance, and the rule of law. For instance, when the KRG imprisoned a diasporic Kurd for criticizing Kurdish president Ma'soud Barzani, pressure from international journalist associations led to his eventual release from jail. Similarly, international criticism of the corruptive practices of the KRG and Kurdish political parties has highlighted the issue of government corruption and the need for transparency in administrative, financial, and political affairs. External actors also should continue to draw attention to these issues, as well as other sociopolitical problems endemic in the Kurdistan Region, such as honor killing, female genital mutilation, violence against children, and killing journalists.

Foreign governments and international organizations also should rethink their one-Iraqi policy as it relates to development of the Kurdish quasi-state. The concern about the Kurdistan Region "becoming too autonomous" and getting ahead of the rest of Iraq is a misguided one that neglects its high levels of underdevelopment, landlocked condition, and institutional weaknesses. It also ignores the logic of quasi-state survival. In doing so, this approach has impeded economic progress in the Kurdistan Region and has fostered resentment among local populations willing to compromise their nationalist agenda for economic gain and political stability. Instead of limiting aid to the Kurdistan Region because it is relatively more stable than the rest of Iraq, foreign governments and donor agencies should seek to maximize the region's economic potential as a means of assuring it will remain part of Iraq. Donor agencies should provide the Kurdistan Region with the same opportunities for economic self-sufficiency and political development as they do for other part of the country, while continuing to assure that the region is an integral part of Iraq.

The continued role of politics in shaping center-periphery relations further underlines the limitations of aid in shaping those relations and the pressing need for a political formula alongside an economic development strategy. That is, even if the Kurdistan Region receives more balanced and accessible aid distributions focused on capacity building, its ties to Baghdad would still be influenced by historical legacies and local politics. Political trust matters, and its absence can negatively influence the noblest efforts of developing lucrative commercial linkages and mechanisms for power, resource, and revenue sharing. If the KRG consistently has to dispute with Baghdad to receive its annual budget or develop petroleum resources, if Baghdad and non-Kurdish communities have to defend their own identities and interests in Kurdish controlled and disputed territories, then it is unlikely that a positive relationship can emerge or be sustained between the regions.

The Kurds may have some legitimate claims about political abuses against them by successive Ba'athist regimes; however, they should also be aware of the discriminatory policies and behavior they have practiced toward non-Kurdish communities, particularly in Kirkuk and the disputed territories, as a means of "re-Kurdifying" and claiming what they perceive is their land. In addition to confidence-building measures between Arbil and Baghdad, and a special status solution for Kirkuk for at least a decade, political trust needs to be fostered at the regional level. The government of Turkey has made important, positive steps toward recognizing the KRG and promoting economic development in the region and should continue in this direction. Similarly, KRG officials should continue to check the PKK issue inside the region, cooperate with Ankara to assure border security and a positive business climate, and protect the rights of Turcoman populations. It also must modify its myopic approach to Kirkuk and appeal to non-Kurdish communities as part of a real power-sharing solution for the city.

The limitations of aid also have implications for the Kurds themselves. The KRG may have been prevented from developing its political economy and engaging in social change during the prewar and early aid periods; however, after 2003, failures in local development—absence of transparency, checks on individual liberties and free speech, and noncommitment to the rule of law—can no longer be blamed on a disinterested international community. With a generous annual budget from Baghdad, and large autonomy and internal sovereigny, the onus of responsibility for economic and political development now lies with the KRG. Large-scale efforts made by foreign governments and international organizations to build the infrastructure in the Kurdistan Region are often obstructed by domestic structural constraints: political culture, historical legacies, and traditional power structures. In fact, some Kurdish officials have rejected opportunities for development and reform proposed by INGOs and donor agencies, opting instead to retain ineffective and inefficient systems of governance and administration, as well as family-run power structures. Local populations also remain attached to tribal and customary law, which precludes the acceptance and implementation of the rule of law.

Indeed, some aid programs, especially the OFFP, reinforced the culture of dependency and tolerated corruption in the Kurdistan Region. The mass infusion of cash into the Kurdish economy without a strategic plan, distribution of food to those who did not need it, and purchase of wheat outside the region encouraged the "Big Daddy syndrome" that defines Kurdish society, while supporting local populations not to work. Still, since 2003 the KRG has allowed this condition to continue by pursuing allocating over 75 percent of the budget to public-sector salaries, failing to develop agro-industry, and refusing to engage in social and political engineering. Kurdish officials have talked convincingly in public about their commitment to democracy and political opening; however, they have permitted the political parties to control the market and institutions, allowed farmlands to remain idle, and assured their own patronage systems.

Instead of blaming the international community for insufficient development assistance, the KRG must assume greater responsibility for its political decisions and their consequences on processes and outcomes. It must check the monopolization of power and resources of the secular nationalist parties and encourage greater political opening. It must tolerate real political opposition and permit challengers to compete equally in the political arena, which includes free and fair elections. It must reduce the dependency of local populations on public handouts and encourage a culture of work and learning. It must minimize gross discrepancies in wealth that have virtually removed the middle class from society while tolerating corruption. It must encourage a culture of tolerance of non-Kurdish communities and their historical and political claims to disputed territories. Unless these domestic constraints are addressed by the Kurdish leadership, no amount of foreign aid can develop the Kurdistan Region in the long term. These local issues pose the greatest challenges to the stability and development of the Kurdish quasi-state, its political autonomy, its legitimacy, and the leverage it can assert in Iraq.

GLOSSARY

REFERENCES

INDEX

Glossary

agha: landowner.

Asaysh: security force (Kurdish).

donum: unit of measurement equivalent to 2,500 square miles (26,910 square feet).

dowry: bride payment.

hawlana system: informal system of loaning money among Kurdish communities based upon personal trust and family ties.

iqta: modern agrarian system defined by patriarchical mechanisms of labor control, such as sharecropping and tenancy on large estates and based on social relations of production. Where customary property rights were weak or where tribesmen could challenge the shaykh, a weaker form of *iqta* emerged, alongside conflict.

jash: traitor; lit., donkey foal.

lasmah tenure: type of land ownership granted to those who have exploited the land for a given period of time; right of settlement and cultivation.

maf: right (Kurdish).

miri: state-owned lands. Under this system of land ownership the state leases land to cultivators by annual contracts based on a crop-sharing system.

mufti: Islamic scholar.

mukhabarat: Iraqi intelligence service.

mustashar: local state official.

nahiyya: subdistrict.

peshmerga: Kurdish militia; lit., those who face death.

qadha: district.

qawmiyya: a form of pan-Arab nationalism based on the premise of a shared Arab national identity.

shaykh: religious official or village leader.

tapu: land tenure established under the Ottoman administration.

waqf: an unincorporated trust under Islamic law by a person for the provision of a designated service in perpetuity.

wasta: personal contacts and influence used to determine decisions and outcomes.

wataniyya: nationalism based on state sovereignty and territory.

References

Abdullah, Çinar Sa'ad. 2005. *Karîgerî Barî Sîyasî leser Geşekırdınî Hôşarî Neteweyî Kûrd dway Raperînî 1991.* Hawler (Arbil): Chapkhaney-î Roşınbırî.

Ahmad, Mahmood. 2002. "Agricultural Policy Issues and Challenges in Iraq: Short and Medium-Term Options." In *Iraq's Economic Predicament,* ed. Kamil A. Madhi, 169–99. Reading, UK: Ithaca Press.

Ahmed, Mohammed M. A. 1993. "The People and Land Resources of Kurdistan-Iraq." Tallahassee: Badlisy Center for Kurdish Studies.

Alkadiri, Raad, and Fareed Mohamedi. 2003. "World Oil Markets and the Invasion of Iraq." *Middle East Report,* no. 227:20–31.

Alnasrawi, Abbas. 1991. *Arab Nationalism, Oil, and the Political Economy of Dependency.* New York: Greenwood Press.

——. 1994. *The Economy of Iraq.* Westport: Greenwood Press.

——. 2001. "Iraq: Economic Sanctions and Consequences, 1990–2000." *Third World Quarterly* 22, no. 2:205–18.

Amara, Hamid Ait. 1987. "The State, Social Classes, and Agricultural Policies in the Arab World." In *The Rentier State,* ed. Hasem Beblawi and Giacomo Luciani, 138–59. London: Croom Helm.

Anderson, Mary B. 1999. *Do No Harm: How Aid Can Support Peace—Or War.* Boulder: Lynne Rienner.

Atlasi Kirkuk. 2006. Aqlim Kurdistan Iraq, Al-Lijna Al Ulia Li Munahaza Ta'arib Kurdistan. Arbil: Mektab Aljamahir Lil Taba'a.

Awena. 2007. "Nerxî kiloyek zir 5 hezar dolar ziadikird." Nov. 13, 5.

Awla, Rasool. 2003. "The Kurdish Civil Society and Its Potential in Iraqi Kurdistan: 1993–1994." In *Democratization and Civil Society in the Middle East: Case Studies of the Palestinian Self-Rule Areas and Iraqi Kurdistan,* ed. Michael Schultz, 216–54. Göteborg, Sweden: Centre for Middle East Studies, Göteborg Univ. .

Bahcheli, Tozun, Barry Bartmann, and Henry Srebrnik, eds. 2004. *De Facto States: The Quest for Sovereignty.* London: Routledge.

141

Ball, Nicole. 1996. *Making Peace Work: The Role of the International Development Community.* Washington, D.C.: Overseas Development Council.

"Ballots Without Borders: A Report on the May 1992 Elections in Iraqi Kurdistan." 1992. Washington, D.C.: International Human Rights Laws Group.

Barakat, Sultan. 2005. "Post-War Reconstruction and Development: Coming of Age." In *After the Conflict: Reconstruction and Development in the Aftermath of War,* ed. Sultan Barakat, 7–32. London: I. B. Tauris.

Barakat, Sultan, and Margaret Chard. 2005. "Building Post-War Capacity: Where to Start?" In *After the Conflict: Reconstruction and Development in the Aftermath of War,* ed. Sultan Barakat, 173–90. London: I. B. Tauris.

Baram, Amatzia. 2000. "The Effect of Iraqi Sanctions: Statistical Pitfalls and Responsibility." *Middle East Journal* 54, no. 2:194-223.

Barkey, Henri J. 2009. *Preventing Conflict Over Kurdistan.* Washington, D.C.: Carnegie Endowment for International Peace.

Barnett, Jon, Beth Eggleston, and Michael Webber. 2003. "Peace and Development in Post-War Iraq." *Middle East Policy* 10, no. 3:22–32.

Barth, Fredrik. 1953. *Principles of Social Organization in Southern Kurdistan.* Brodrene Jorgensen A/S: Oslo.

Barwari, Muhammed. 2002. "Iqtisad Iqleem Kurdistan wal Iraq: Tabaz um Takumul?" *Althaqafa Al-Jadeeda,* no. 305:69-74.

Barzani, Hoshyar. 1995. "Les élites parlementaires Kurdes Irakiennes." Maitrise de sociologie, Université Lumière de Lyon II.

Batatu, Hanna. 1979. *The Old Social Classes and the Revolutionary Movements in Iraq.* Princeton: Princeton Univ. Press.

Belgrade, Eric and Nitza Nachmias, eds. 1997. *The Politics of International Humanitarian Aid Operations.* Westport: Praeger.

Benini, Aldo, Charles Conley, Joseph Donahue, and Shawn Messick. 2005. "Challenges of Humanitarian Information Management in Iraq." *Sociological Focus* 39, no. 4:285–300.

Berman, Sheri. 2001. "Civil Society and Political Institutionalization." In *Beyond Tocqueville: Civil Society and the Social Capital Debate in Comparative Perspective,* ed. Bob Edwards, Michael W. Foley, and Mario Diani, 32–42. Hanover, N.H.: Univ. Press of New England.

Billet, Bret L. 1993. *Modernization Theory and Economic Development: Discontent in the Developing World.* Westport: Praeger.

Blomberg, S. Brock, and Gregory D. Hess. 2002. "The Temporal Links Between Conflict and Economic Activity." *Journal of Conflict Resolution* 46, no. 1:74–90.

Bookman, Milica Zarkovic. 1991. *The Political Economy of Discontinuous Development.* New York: Praeger.

Bozarslan, Hamit. 1996. "Kurdistan: Économie de Guerre, Économie Dans La Guerre." In *Économie des guerres civiles,* ed. François Jean and Jean-Christophe Rufin, 105–46. Paris: Hachette.

Bratton, Michael, and Nicolas van de Walle. 1997. *Democratic Experiments in Africa: Regime Transitions in Comparative Perspective.* Cambridge: Cambridge Univ. Press.

Brown, Mark Malloch. 2003. "Democratic Governance: Toward a Framework for Sustainable Peace." *Global Governance* 9, no. 2:141–46.

Brynan, Rex. 2000. *A Very Political Economy: Peacebuilding and Foreign Aid in the West Bank and Gaza.* Washington, D.C.: U.S. Institute of Peace Press.

Calvert, Peter, and Susan Calvert. 2007. *Politics and Society in the Developing World.* Harlow, UK: Pearson Education Limited.

Carapico, Sheila. 2002. "Foreign Aid for Promoting Democracy in the Arab World." *Middle East Journal* 56, no. 3:379–95.

Cemawar. 2007. "Ley kobuneweyekî na asayi 15 madey bô reshnusî destur ziad krawa." Apr. 2, 1, 12.

Chaudry, Kiren Aziz. 2002. "Consuming Interests, Market Failure, and the Social Foundations of Iraqi Etatism." In *Iraq's Economic Predicament,* ed. Kamil A. Mahdi, 233–65. Reading, UK: Ithaca Press.

Chehabi, H. E. 1997. "Ardabil Becomes a Province: Center-Periphery Relations in Iran." *International Journal of Middle East Studies* 29, no. 2:235–43.

Chorev, Matan. 2007. "Iraqi Kurdistan: The Internal Dynamics and Statecraft of a Semi-state." Master's thesis, Tufts Univ., MALD, Boston, Mass.

Collier, Paul. 2002. "Social Capital and Poverty: A Microeconomic Perspective." In *The Role of Social Capital in Development: An Empirical Assessment,* ed. Christian Grootaert and Thierry van Bastelaer, 19–41. Cambridge: Cambridge Univ. Press.

Collier, Paul, et. al. 2003. *Breaking the Conflict Trap: Civil War and Development Policy.* Washington, D.C.: International Bank for Reconstruction and Development.

Committee to Protect Journalists. 2009. cpj.org/2009/03/iraqi-paper-former-editor-fined-for-defaming-presi.php.

Costello, V. F. 1977. *Urbanization in the Middle East.* Cambridge: Cambridge Univ. Press.

Crusoe, Jonathan. 1986. "Economic Outlook: Guns and Butter, Phase Two?" In *Iraq in Transition: A Political, Economic, and Strategic Perspective,* ed. Frederick Axelgard, 33–58. Boulder, Colo.: Westview Press.

Dahiri, Abdul Wahab M. al-. 1976. *Economics of the Agricultural Sector in Iraq.* Baghdad: Univ. of Baghdad.

Davis, Eric. 2005. "The Uses of Historical Memory." *Journal of Democracy* 16, no. 3:54–68.

Deely, Sean. 2005. "War, Health, and Recovery." In *After the Conflict: Reconstruction and Development in the Aftermath of War,* ed. Sultan Barakat, 123–39. London: I. B. Tauris.

DiPrizio, Robert C. 2002. *Armed Humanitarians: U.S. Interventions from Northern Iraq to Kosovo.* Baltimore: Johns Hopkins Univ. Press.

Duarte, Mafalda. 2003. *Aid Policy in War-Torn Countries.* Lanham, Md.: Univ. Press of America.

Dube, S. C. 1988. *Modernization and Development: The Search for Alternative Paradigms.* London and Tokyo: Zed Books and United Nations Univ.

Duffield, Mark. 2001. *Global Governance and the New Wars.* London: Zed Books.

Edîb, Mohsin. 2001. *Paş Raperîn oo Pisekanî Komelî Medenî.* Suleymaniya: Nawendî Roşınbırî Bedlisî.

ELKLM. 1992. "Electing the Leader of the Kurdistan Liberation Movement." Arbil (Hawler): Kurdistan Regional Government.

ELKNA. 1992. "Electoral Law for the Kurdistan National Assembly." Arbil (Hawler): Kurdistan Regional Government.

Emin, Hadi. 2008. "Berwarad bey welatanî pishkewtu jimarey-î qutabî bô mamusta ley herimî Kurdistan berejeh-î ley seda shesht ziatereh." *Hawlati,* Jan. 13, 8.

Encarnacion, Omar G. 2003. *The Myth of Civil Society: Social Capital and Democratic Consolidation in Spain and Brazil.* Houndmills, UK: Palgrave Macmillan.

Entelis, John P. 2005. "The Democratic Imperative vs. the Authoritarian Impulse: The Maghrib State Between Transition and Terrorism." *Middle East Journal* 59, no. 4:537–58.

FAO (Food and Agriculture Organization Representation in Iraq). 2002. "Rural Socioeconomic Survey of the Iraqi Northern Governorates of Dohuk, Arbil, and Suleimaniyah." Arbil: FAO Coordination Office for Northern Iraq.

———. 2003. "Annual Statistical Bulletin no. 4, year 2002." Arbil: FAO Coordination Office for Northern Iraq.

Fischer-Tahir, Andreya. 2009. *Brave Men, Pretty Women? Gender and Symbolic Violence in Iraqi Kurdish Urban Society.* Berlin: Europaisches Zentrum fur Kurdische Studien.

Fukayama, Francis. 1995. *Trust: The Social Virtues and the Creation of Prosperity.* London: Hamish Hamilton.

———. 2002. "Social Capital and Development: The Coming Agenda." *SAIS Review* 22, no. 1:23–37.

Gazdar, Harris, and Athar Hussain. 2002. "Crisis and Response: A Study of the Impact of Economic Sanctions on Iraq." In *Iraq's Economic Predicament,* ed. Kamil A. Mahdi, 31–83. Reading, UK: Ithaca Press.

Gerdi, Aziz. 2005. *Rowşî Aburî oo Komelayetî-yi Kurdî Rowanduz*. Suleymaniya: Chap-khaney-î Rûn.

Gounder, Rukmani. 2002. "Empirical Evidence of the Relationship Between Foreign Aid and Economic Growth: The Case of the Solomon Islands." In *New Perspectives on Foreign Aid and Economic Development*, ed. B. Mak Arvin, 141–69. Westport: Praeger.

Graham-Brown, Sarah. 1999. *Sanctioning Saddam: The Politics of Intervention in Iraq*. London: I. B Tauris.

———. 2002. "Humanitarian Needs and International Assistance in Iraq after the Gulf War." In *Iraq's Economic Predicament*, ed. Kamil A. Mahdi, 267–88. Reading, UK: Ithaca Press.

Griffiths, Hugh. 1999. "A Political Economy of Ethnic Conflict: Ethno-nationalism and Organised Crime." *Civil Wars* 2, no. 2:56–73.

Grootaert, Christiaan, and Thierry van Bastelaer, eds. 2002. *The Role of Social Capital in Development: An Empirical Assessment*. Cambridge: Cambridge Univ. Press.

Haj, Samira. 1997. *The Making of Iraq 1900–1963: Capital, Power, and Ideology*. Albany: State Univ. of New York Press.

Hasan, Mohammad Salman. 1970. "The Role of Foreign Trade in the Economic Development of Iraq, 1864–1964: A Study in the Growth of Dependent Economy." In *Studies in the Economic History of the Middle East*, ed. M. A. Cook, 346–72. London: Oxford Univ. Press.

Haseeb, K. 1964. *The National Income of Iraq: 1953–1961*. London: Oxford Univ. Press.

Hawlati. 2007a. "Bey hoy-î dakhestenî merzekaneweh herimî Kurdistan rojaneh yek million dolar zianî leydekeweyt," Sept. 26, 2.

———. 2007b. "Budjey-î hakumetî herimî bo sali 2008 hewt milyar dolar." Oct. 3, 3.

Hay, W. R. 1921. *Two Years in Kurdistan*. London: Sidgwick and Jackson.

Herring, Eric, and Glen Rangwala. 2006. *Iraq in Fragments: The Occupation and Its Legacy*. Ithaca: Cornell Univ. Press.

Hiltermann, Joost R. 2007. *A Poisonous Affair: America, Iraq, and the Gassing of Halabja*. Cambridge: Cambridge Univ. Press.

Hoff, Ruud, Michiel Leezenberg, and Peter Muller. 1992. *Elections in Iraqi Kurdistan: An Experiment in Democracy*. The Hague: Pax Christi International.

Hooghe, Marc, and Dietlind Stolle. 2003. "Introduction: Generating Social Capital." In *Generating Social Capital: Civil Society and Institutions in Comparative Perspective*, ed. Marc Hooghe and Dietlind Stolle, 1–8. New York: Palgrave Macmillan.

Hout, Wil. 2004. "Political Regimes and Development Assistance: The Political Economy of Aid Selectivity." *Critical Asian Studies* 36, no. 4:591–613.

Hudson, Michael C. 1994. "Arab Regimes and Democratization: Responses and the Challenge of Political Islam." *International Spectator* 29, no. 4:3–27.

Hussain, Abdullah Krekar. 2000. *Keştukal oo biryarî 987.* Slimani: Chapkhaney Renj.

IBRD (International Bank for Reconstruction and Development). 1952. *The Economic Development of Iraq.* Report. Baltimore: Johns Hopkins Univ. Press.

ICG. 2006. "Iraq and the Kurds: The Brewing Battle over Kirkuk." Middle East Report no. 56, International Crisis Group, Brussels.

———. 2010. "Iraq's Uncertain Future: Elections and Beyond." Middle East Report no. 94, International Crisis Group, Brussels.

ICRC. 2007. "Mission Report: Iraqi-Kurdistan Region Livelihood Program." Arbil: International Committee of the Red Cross.

ILCS. 2005. "Iraq Living Conditions Survey: 2004." Vols. 1–3. Baghdad: Central Organization for Statistics and Information Technology, Ministry of Planning and Development Cooperation.

Inglehart, Ronald. 1997. *Modernization and Postmodernization: Cultural, Economic, and Political Change in 43 Societies.* Princeton: Princeton Univ. Press.

Iraq Household Socio-Economic Survey (IHSES). 2008. *Central Organization for Statistics and Information Technology.* Amman: National Press.

Issawi, Charles. 1966. *The Economic History of the Middle East 1800-1914.* Chicago: Univ. of Chicago Press.

Iversen, Carl. 1954. *Monetary Policy in Iraq.* Copenhagen: Nordlunges Bogtrykkeri.

Jackson, Robert. H. 1990. *Quasi States: Sovereignty, International Relations, and the Third World.* Cambridge: Cambridge Univ. Press.

Jean, François. 1996. "Aide Humanitaire et Economie de Guerre." In *Economie des Guerres Civiles,* ed. François Jean and Jean-Christophe Rufin, 543–89. Paris: Hachette.

Jean, François, and Jean-Christophe Rufin. 1996. *Economie des Guerres Civiles.* Paris: Hachette.

Jones, Richard. 2005. "The Economics of War and Post-Conflict Poverty Reduction." In *After the Conflict: Reconstruction and Development in the Aftermath of War,* ed. Sultan Barakat, 101–22. London: I. B. Tauris.

JRI-KS. 2006. "Judicial Reform Index for Iraq: Kurdistan Supplement." Iraqi Legal Development Project. Washington, D.C.: American Bar Association.

Katzman, Kenneth. 2005. "Iraq: U.S. Regime Change Efforts and Post-Saddam Governance." Washington, D.C.: Congressional Research Service, Library of Congress.

Khadduri, Majid. 1978. *Socialist Iraq: A Study in Iraqi Politics Since 1968.* Washington, D.C.: Middle East Institute.

Khorshid, Fuad Hama. 2005. *Kirkuk Qalb-e Kurdistan.* Suleymaniya: General Directorate for Printing and Publishing, Ministry of Culture, Kurdistan Regional Government, No. 358 (in Arabic).

Khudayri, Tariq al-. 2002. "Iraq's Manufacturing Industry: Status and Prospects for
Rehabiliations and Reform." In *Iraq's Economic Predicament,* ed. Kamil A. Mahdi,
201–29. Reading, UK: Ithaca Press.

King, Charles. 2001. "The Benefits of Ethnic War: Understanding Eurasia's Unrecognized
States." *World Politics* 53:524–52.

Kirk, Alistair, and Gary Sawdon. 2002. "Understanding Kurdish Livelihoods in Northern
Iraq: Final Report." London: The Northern Iraq Country Programme and the Food
Security and Livelihoods Unit, Save the Children, (UK).

Knack, Stephen. 2004. "Does Foreign Aid Promote Democracy?" *International Studies
Quarterly* 48:251–66.

Kolsto, Pål. 2006. "The Sustainability and Future of Unrecognized Quasi-States." *Journal
of Peace Research* 43, no 6:723–740.

Kopp, Pierre. 1996. "Embargo et Criminalisation de L'Economie." In *Economie des guerres
civiles,* ed. François Jean and Jean-Christophe Rufin. 425–65. Paris: Hachette.

KRG. 2006. "Kurdistan Regional Government Unification Agreement." Jan. 21. www
.krg.org/articles/detail.asp?smap=02010100&lngnr=12&asnr=&anr=8891&rnr=223.

KRG-MOE (Kurdistan Regional Government, Ministry of Education). 2009. "Basic and
Secondary Education School System." Arbil: Kurdistan Region of Iraq.

———. 2010. "Basic and Secondary Education School System." Arbil: Kurdistan Region
of Iraq.

KRG-MOI (Kurdistan Regional Government, Ministry of Industry). 2007. "Establishment of Privatization Projects, 2001–2006." Arbil: Kurdistan Region of Iraq.

Krishna, Anirudh. 2002. *Active Social Capital: Tracing the Roots of Development and
Democracy.* New York: Columbia Univ. Press.

Kuran, Timur. 2004. "Why the Middle East is Economically Underdeveloped: Historical
Mechanisms of Institutional Stagnation." *Journal of Economic Perspectives* 18, no
3:71–90.

"Kurdistan PM's Speech: With Investors' Help We'll Be Producers Again." 2006. www.
peyamner.com, Nov. 12, 2.

Langley, Kathleen. 1961. *The Industrialization of Iraq.* Cambridge, Mass.: Harvard Univ.
Press.

Larrain Rios, Guillermo. 2005. "Croissance Rapide et Inégalités Extrêmes au Chili." *Prob-
lemès D'Amérique Latine* 56:81–101.

Leca, Jean. 1990. "Social Structure and Political Stability: Comparative Evidence from the Algerian, Syrian, and Iraqi Cases." In *The Arab State,* ed. Luciani Giacomo, 150–88. Berkeley: Univ. of California Press.

Leezenberg, Michiel. 1999. "Refugee Camp or Free Trade Zone? The Economy of Iraqi Kurdistan Since 1991." In *Iraq's Economic Predicament,* ed. Kamil A. Mahdi, 289–319. Reading, UK: Ithaca Press.

Looney, Robert. 1992. "Economic Development in Iraq: Factors Underlying the Relative Deterioration of Human Capital Formation." *Journal of Economic Issues* 26, no. 2:615–22.

———. 2003a. "A Monetary/Exchange-Rate Strategy for the Reconstruction of Iraq." *Middle East Policy* 10, no. 3:33–42.

———. 2003b. "The Neoliberal Model's Planned Role in Iraq's Economic Transition." *Middle East Journal* 57, no. 4:568-86.

MacLean, Ken. 2004. "Reconfiguring the Debate on Engagement: Burmese Exiles and the Changing Politics of Aid." *Critical Asian Studies* 36, no. 3:323–54.

Macrae, Joanna. 2001. *Aiding Recovery?: The Crisis of Aid in Chronic Political Emergencies.* London: Zed Books.

Mahdi, Kamil A., ed. 2002. *Iraq's Economic Predicament.* Reading, UK: Ithaca Press.

Marr, Phebe. 1985. *The Modern History of Iraq.* Boulder, Colo.: Westview Press.

McQueen, Carol. 2005. *Humanitarian Intervention and Safety Zones: Iraq, Bosnia, and Rwanda.* Basingstoke, UK: Palgrave Macmillan.

MERA. 2007. "Report on the Administrative Changes in Kirkuk and the Disputed Regions." Oct. Arbil: Kurdistan Regional Government, Ministry of Extra Regional Affairs.

Milas, Seifulaziz, and Jalal Abdel Latif. 2000. "The Political Economic of Complex Emergency and Recovery in Northern Ethiopia." *Disasters* 24, no. 4:363–79.

Mohammed, Awat, and Ahmad, Hedi. 2007. "Chwarqorneh 46 sal ziadtera nahiyeh-ye key chi heshta tapu-yî niya." *Hawleti,* Nov. 28.

Mohammed, Simko Behruz. 2005. *Mîjoo-i serdemeh kargirî u berweberiyekanî parêzga-i Kirkuk.* Kirkuk: Chapkhaney-i Shehid Azad Hawrami.

Mosse, David. 2005. "Global Governance and the Ethnography of International Aid." In *The Aid Effect,* ed. David Mosse and David Lewis, 1–36. London: Pluto Press.

Muscat, Robert. 2002. *Investing in Peace: How Development Aid Can Prevent or Promote Conflict.* Armonk, N.Y.: M. E. Sharpe.

MWIA. 2000. "Chalakî u projekanî wezareti awqaf u karubarî islamî taybet bey drut kirden u chakirdeneweyî mizgewt u tekiyya u qutabkhaneyî islamî u balakhaneykanî wezaret." Serkurdayetî Enjumanî Wezaran, Wezareti Awqaf u Karubarî Islamî, Hakumet Herimî Kurdistan, Iraq.

————. 2006. "Prôjekani wezareti karubari ayini 2000-2004, Hawler u Dohuk." Serkurd-ayeti Enjumani Wezaran, Wezareti Awqaf u Karubari Islami, Hakumet Herimi Kurdistan, Iraq.

Natali, Denise. 1999. "Humanitarian Aid, Regional Politics, and the Kurdish Issue in Iraq since the Persian Gulf War." Situation Paper No. 31, Emirates Center for Strategic Studies and Research. Abu Dhabi.

————. 2001. "Manufacturing Identity and Managing Kurds in Iraq." In *Rightsizing the State: The Politics of Moving Borders,* ed. Brendan O'Leary, Ian S. Lustick, and Thomas Callaghy, 252–88. London: Oxford Univ. Press.

————. 2005. *The Kurds and the State: Evolving National Identity in Iraq, Turkey, and Iran.* Syracuse: Syracuse Univ. Press.

————. 2007. "The Spoils of Peace in Iraqi Kurdistan." *Third World Quarterly* 28, no. 6:1111–29.

————. 2008. "The Kirkuk Conundrum." *Ethnopolitics* 7, no. 4 (Nov. 2008): 433–43.

Nijman, Jan. 2002. "The Effects of Economic Globalization: Land Use and Land Values in Mumbai, India." In *Globalization and the Margins,* ed. Richard Grant and John Rennie Short, 151–69. Basingstoke: Palgrave Macmillan.

North, Douglass C. 1990. *Institutions, Institutional Change, and Economic Performance.* Cambridge: Cambridge Univ. Press.

ODHD. 2007. "Overview of Directorate of Health/Dohuk Governorate." Dohuk Province: Directorate of Health, Dohuk Governorate, Organization Coordination Office.

Olson, Robert. 2005. *The Goat and the Butcher: Nationalism and State Formation in Kurd-istan-Iraq since the Iraqi War.* Costa Mesa, Calif.: Mazda.

Özerdem, Alpaslan, and Gianni Rufini. 2005. "Humanitarianism and the Principles of Humanitarian Action in a Post–Cold War Context." In *After the Conflict: Recon-struction and Development in the Aftermath of War,* ed. Sultan Barakat, 51–66. London: I. B. Tauris.

Page, John, and Linda van Gelder. 2001. "Missing Links: Institutional Capability, Pol-icy Reform, and Growth in the Middle East and North Africa." In *The State and Global Change: The Political Economy of Transition in the Middle East and North Africa,* ed. Hassan Hakimian and Ziba Moshaver, 15–58. Richmond, Surrey: Cur-zon Press.

Peck, Connie. 1998. *Sustainable Peace: The Role of the UN and Regional Organizations in Preventing Conflict.* Lanham, Md.: Rowman and Littlefield.

Pollack, David. 2008. "The Kurdish Regional Government in Iraq: An Inside Story." In *The Future of Iraqi Kurds,* ed. Soner Cagaptay, 2–11. Washington, D.C.: Washington Institute for Near East Policy.

Prendergast, John. 1996. *Frontline Diplomacy: Humanitarian Aid and Conflict in Africa.* Boulder: Lynne Rienner.

Pugh, Michael. 2002. "Postwar Political Economy in Bosnia and Herzegovina: The Spoils of Peace." *Global Governance* 8, no. 4:467–82.

Qubain, Fahim Issa. 1958. *The Reconstruction of Iraq: 1950–1957.* London: Atlantic Books.

Reilly, Benjamin, and Robert Phillpot. 2002. "Making Democracy Work in Papua New Guinea: Social Capital and Provincial Development in an Ethnically Fragmented Society." *Asian Survey* 42, no. 6:906–27.

Roberts, J. Timmons, and Amy Hite, eds. 2000. *From Modernization to Globalization: Perspectives on Development and Social Change.* Oxford: Blackwell.

Rondinelli, Dennis A. 1987. *Development Administration and U.S. Foreign Aid Policy.* Boulder: Lynne Rienner.

Ruttan, Vernon W. 1996. *United States Development Assistance Policy: The Domestic Politics of Foreign Economic Aid.* Baltimore: Johns Hopkins Univ. Press.

Rwanin. 2006. "Ley kolejî zeman enjam nedanî gêştî zanastî mangirtinî qutabianî lêkewteweh." May 5, 2.

Safa, Helen I. 1982. *Towards a Political Economy of Urbanization in Third World Countries.* Delhi: Oxford Univ. Press.

Schlumberger, Oliver. 2000. "Arab Political Economy and the European Union's Mediterranean Policy: What Prospects for Development?" *New Political Economy* 5, no. 2:247–68.

———. 2006. "Dancing with Wolves: Dilemmas of Democracy Promotion in Authoritarian Contexts." In *Democratization and Development,* ed. Jung Dietrich, 33–60. Basingstoke, UK: Palgrave Macmillan.

Sharpe, Jeremy M. 2005. "U.S. Foreign Assistance to the Middle East: Historical Background, Recent Trends, and the FY2006 Request." Washington, D.C.: Congressional Research Service, Library of Congress.

Sharpe, Jeremy M., and Christopher M. Blanchard. 2005. "Post-War Iraq: A Table and Chronology of Foreign Contributions." Washington, D.C.: Congressional Research Service, Library of Congress.

Sinha, Aseema. 2003. "Rethinking the Developmental State Model: Divided Leviathan and Subnational Comparisons in India." *Comparative Politics* 35, no. 4:459–76.

Sliman, Muhammed. 2002. "Bazarganî Derekî Herim le 1993 ta 2000." *Eburî Siasî* 1, no. 1:137–48.

Smelser, Neil J. 1971. "Mechanisms of Change and Adjustment to Change." In *Economic Development and Social Change: The Modernization of Village Communities,* ed. George Dalton, 352–74. Garden City, N.Y.: Natural History Press.

Smolansky, Oles M., and B. M. Smolansky. 1991. *The USSR and Iraq: The Soviet Quest for Influence*. Durham: Duke University Press.

Stansfield, Gareth. 2003a. *Iraqi Kurdistan: Political Development and Emergent Democracy*. London: Routledge Curzon.

———. 2003b. "The Kurdish Dilemma: The Golden Era Threatened." In *Iraq at the Crossroads: State and Society in the Shadow of Regime Change*, ed. Toby Dodge and Steven Simon, 131–48. Oxford: Oxford Univ. Press.

Stork, Joe. 1979. "Oil and the Penetration of Capitalism in Iraq: An Interpretation." In *Oil and Business in Iraq, Centre de Recherches sur le Monde Arabe Contemporaine*, Cahier 4, 38–77. Louvain la-Neuve: Institut des Pays en Developpment, Univ. Catholoque de Louvain.

Suhrke, Astri, and Arne Strand. 2005. "The Logic of Conflictual Peacebuilding." In *After the Conflict: Reconstruction and Development in the Aftermath of War*, ed. Sultan Barakat, 142–54. London: I. B. Tauris.

Şwani, Ako Abdulkerim. 2002. *Şarî Slimanî. 1918–1932: lêykôlîneweyekî mijoo-ıyi siasî-ye*. Suleymaniya. Chapkhaney Zanest.

Talabani, Nuri. 1993. "Derbarey-î projey-î desturî herimî Kurdistanî Iraq." London: Kurdish Cultural Center.

———. 2004. *Arabization of the Kirkuk Region*. Arbil: Aras Press.

Tarnoff, Curt. 2004. "Iraq: Recent Developments in Reconstruction Assistance." Washington, D.C.: Congressional Research Service, Library of Congress.

Taysi, Tanyel. 2009. "Eliminating Violence Against Women: Perspectives on Honor-Related Violence in the Iraqi Kurdistan Region: Suleymaniya Governorate." www.uniraq.org/documents/asuda_report_5jun2009.pdf.

THCSEK. 1992. "The High Committee for the Supervision of the Elections in Kurdistan: Election Results, Electoral Law for the Kurdistan National Assembly." Arbil (Hawler).

Thörlind, Robert. 2000. *Development and Decentralization and Democracy: Exploring Social Capital and Politicization in the Bengal Region*. Copenhagen: Nordic Institute of Asian Studies.

Tripp, Charles. 2004. "The United States and State-Building in Iraq." *Review of International Studies* 30:545–58.

———. 2007. *A History of Iraq*. Cambridge: Cambridge Univ. Press.

UNICEF. 1998. Iraq Annual Report. Country Office Annual Reports.

UNICEF. 1999. Iraq Annual Report. Country Office Annual Reports.

UNICEF. 2000. Iraq Annual Report. Country Office Annual Reports.

UNICEF. 2001. Iraq Annual Report. Country Office Annual Reports.

UNICEF. 2002. Iraq Annual Report. Country Office Annual Reports.

UNICEF. 2004. Iraq Annual Report. Country Office Annual Reports.

UNSAI. 2004. "A Strategy for Assistance to Iraq." IRFFI Meeting in Abu Dhabi, Feb. 28.

USAID. 2003. Iraqi Humanitarian and Reconstruction Assistance Fact Sheet, no. 20. U.S. Department of State, Washington, D.C.

USAID/IRAQ. 2008. "Kurdistan Region: Economic Development Assessment." Research Triangle International/USAID, Local Governance Project. Arbil, Iraq.

USGAKR. 2006. U.S. Embassy Baghdad Report. Nov. 31. Baghdad.

Volcker, Paul A., Richard J. Goldstone, and Mark Pieth. 2005. *The Management of the Oil-for-Food Programme*. Vols. 3–4. Independent Inquiry Committee.

Way, Lucan A. 2004. "The Sources and Dynamics of Competitive Authoritarianism in Ukraine." *Journal of Communist Studies and Transition Politics* 20, no. 1:143–61.

WFP. 2004. "Baseline Food Security Analysis of Iraq." United Nations World Food Programme, WFP Iraq Country Office.

Wiarda, Howard J. 2004. *Political Development in Emerging Nations*. Belmont, Calif.: Wadsworth.

Xwendin-i Libral. 2006. "Genjbinî mergî genj." May 8, 3.

Yapp, M. E. 1987. *The Making of the Modern Middle East: 1792–1923*. London: Longman.

"Yasa wazareti perwerdeh." Perleman, no. 2 (Perleman 2). 1992. Arbil (Hawler): Kurdistan Regional Government

Zaborowski, Marcin. 2005. "Westernizing the East: External Influences in the Post-Communist Transformation of Eastern and Central Europe." *Journal of Communist Studies and Transition Politics* 21, no. 1:16–32.

Zaher-Draey, Rasheda. 2005. "An Overview of English Language Teaching in Kurdistan." *Global Issues* (IATEFL CISIG Newsletter) 17, no. 17:36–40.

Zetter, Roger. 2005. "Land, Housing, and the Reconstruction of the Built Environment." In *After the Conflict: Reconstruction and Development in the Aftermath of War*, ed. Sultan Barakat, 155–72. London: I. B. Tauris.

Index